The Language of Love

The Language of Love

Exploring Prayer: An Anthology

John Moses

CANTERBURY
PRESS
Norwich

© in this compilation John Moses 2007

First published in 2007 by The Canterbury Press Norwich
(a publishing imprint of Hymns Ancient & Modern
Limited, a registered charity)
13–17 Long Lane, London ECIA 9PN

www.scm-canterburypress.co.uk

British Library Cataloguing in Publication data

A catalogue record for this book is available
from the British Library

ISBN 978-1-85311-783-1

Typeset by Regent Typesetting, London
Printed and bound by
MPG Books Ltd, Bodmin, Cornwall

Contents

FOR VINCENT AND NINA

From quiet homes and first beginning,
Out to the undiscovered ends,
There's nothing worth the wear of of winning,
But laughter and the love of friends.

Hilaire Belloc, 'Dedicatory Ode', Verses, 1910

Acknowledgements

I am glad to acknowledge the permission that has been granted to quote from many published works in the compilation of this anthology. Every attempt has been made to secure permission to use copyright material, and all such material is acknowledged in the Notes at the end of the book.

I am also glad to acknowledge the support I have received over many years from SCM-Canterbury Press and especially in recent years from Mrs Christine Smith, with whom it has been good to work from the beginning in the preparation of this book.

Nothing could have been achieved, however, without the untiring efforts of Mrs Nicola Quy, who was my Private Secretary during my final years at St Paul's and who helped enormously in preparing the manuscript for publication.

Preface

Theory and practice are two different things. It is easy to speak of prayer in the context of Christian discipleship as encounter, dialogue, engagement; but the practice – or the absence of a consistent, developing and mature practice – of personal prayer is a different matter. Prayer comes so easily into the category of 'things I suppose I ought to do'.[1]

There is no dissent from Thomas Ken's counsel that 'prayer is the very life of a Christian',[2] but the actual experience of praying is so often perfunctory, predictable. We throw ourselves into life. Indeed, we spend a good deal of our lives assembling building blocks – relationships, work, skills, hobbies, families, friendships, cultural pursuits; but there is no strong sense that prayer gives connectedness, focus, stability to the miscellaneous and unrelated aspects of our existence. Prayer is something that is either removed from everyday life or is imposed upon it.

There are the inevitable contradictions between how we live and what we pray; and yet we are driven back time and again to prayer.

> To be alive then
> was to be aware how necessary
> prayer was and impossible.[3]

But why should it be impossible? Or could it be that we are feeling after an entirely new understanding of what prayer means? 'Prayer seeks to break new ground. Prayer wants a world made new. Prayer tries to find its own authentic voice.'[4]

New perceptions, new horizons can be dangerously deceptive. The Gospel injunction remains: 'Every scribe who is trained for the kingdom of heaven is like a householder who brings out of his treasury what is new and what is old.'[5] I find it difficult nonetheless to ignore the observation made thirty years ago by Alan Ecclestone in his book *Yes to God*: 'For far too long the Christian world has lived at ease with its faith, assumed too lightly that it knew how to pray, and dealt too carelessly with the stuff out of which prayer is to be made.'[6] So what is the stuff out of which prayer is made? What are the things old and new which we are asked to bring out of our treasury?

Two insights concerning the meaning of prayer have mattered to me over the years.

First, there is the recognition that prayer is 'God's activity in us'.[7] Prayer is not in the first instance something we do. It is the response – tentative, diffident, unfocussed – to what we have seen or heard or felt. George Herbert speaks of prayer as 'God's breath in man returning to his birth'.[8] The initiative in prayer remains with God. Prayer is His work in us. It is not we who pray to God. It is He who prays in us. This is why it is possible to say that 'we enter God's energy when we pray'.[9]

Secondly, there is the discovery that prayer is the 'language of love'.[10] An awareness of the emptiness of our prayers should not necessarily lead to the questions: Do I really believe in God? Am I losing my faith? Does prayer make any difference? It might be more helpful to address other questions: Do I love? What or whom do I love? How much do I love? Prayer expresses – or should it be exposes? – our capacity for love. 'Our ability to love is our ability to pray.'[11]

It is these two insights concerning the meaning of prayer that are exemplified supremely in the Gospels. There are times in all four Gospels when Jesus is manifestly at prayer: the nights spent on the hills alone with the Father; the Garden of Gethsemane. But no reading of the Gospels could ever suggest that there was *any* time in His public ministry when Jesus was not actually praying. His passionate engagement with the Father and with all around Him is an unbroken life of prayer; and what is demonstrated time and again is the truth that prayer is both 'God's activity in us'[12] and the 'language of love'.[13]

The inferences that might be drawn from these two insights are commonplace. They are reflections that have been made time and again by writers of books about prayer. The exploration of prayer cannot be separated from the exploration of discipleship. Prayer cannot be confined to times of prayer. Prayer is open, inclusive, all-embracing. Prayer is inescapably bound up with the search for direction, focus, meaning.

Prayer requires a far broader definition than its popular stereotypes would suggest. There is nothing that can ever detach the prayer of the Christian from the life of the Church and its tradition of public corporate prayer. 'Christian prayer is part of our being in Christ.'[14] Nor is there any thought that a wholehearted engagement with life can remove the necessity of going into a room by ourselves, shutting the door, and praying to our Father who is in secret.[15]

It is nonetheless within the everyday life of our humanity that we must find the arena where these two things – prayer as the divine activity and prayer as the language of love – can be discerned, explored, lived out. But these two things are one. The divine activity *is* the language of love; and because we are far more easily aware in our daily routines of loving and of being loved (or of not loving and of not being loved) than we are of the divine activity, it has seemed right to take prayer as the language of love as our way into an understanding of the meaning of the practice of prayer.

The starting point for an exploration of prayer as the language of love can only be the biblical and theological tradition within which we stand as Christian people. Love – we are reminded – is the power in which the divine life has been lived from before the foundation of the world.[16] Love is the power in which the divine life gives itself to the world.[17] Love is the power which loves its own and loves to the end.[18] Love is the power by which the Son lays down His life for us.[19] Love is the power by which we pass from death to life.[20] Love is the power from which nothing in all creation will be able to separate us.[21]

What these words provide is an unambiguous affirmation of the strength and stability of the divine love: its indestructibility, its self-giving, its patience, its vulnerability, its capacity 'to bear all things, believe all things, hope all things, endure all things'.[22]

But does prayer as the language of love ask that we come nearer home? Is it possible to move from an understanding of the love which is the life of God to an experience of love which is an inescapable part of our humanity? Is the Song of Songs, for example, with its portrayal of human love, erotic love, sexual love, an appropriate analogy of God's dealings with His people? Or are the instances of deprivation, manipulation and abuse so frequent and so grotesque that we cannot slip into an exploration of love as the language of prayer without being grievously misunderstood? Or could it be that love as the Christian tradition understands it, and the ideal of love to which we aspire even as we sell ourselves short, is the universal currency in which we might properly trade if we want to come to a fuller understanding of the meaning and practice of prayer?

What, then, are the primary characteristics of both divine and human love? Is it not that love gives and love receives; that love connects; that love softens, deepens, refreshes, enlarges, energizes, renews; that love makes whole, makes one? And are not these precisely the characteristics that we find in the face and in the behaviour of those who pray?

The experience of human love is necessarily diverse. There are aspects of loving and of being loved that are not accommodated within the template of this anthology; but prayer – *because it is the language of love* – encompasses awareness, exploration, passion, pain, patience, companionship, abandonment. These are the words that are most easily recognized as the distinguishing marks of our experience.

These key aspects, which correspond to our experience of making, establishing, maintaining and letting go of loving relationships, do not necessarily present themselves in a predictably chronological sequence. They stand in relation to each other and take their place within the total experience of loving and of being loved.

Awareness might lead to exploration, and exploration to passion, and passion to pain, and so on; but exploration can by-pass passion and lead directly to companionship; pain might require us to go back to the beginning and learn the meaning of awareness and exploration all over again; abandonment will be present in some form or another – a letting go, a handing over – long before that final physical separation which is imposed by death. And some of these key aspects will also appear simultaneously: passion and pain can go hand in hand; exploration and patience most certainly require each other; companionship presupposes a continuing and unselfconscious awareness.

There will be time enough in the course of this anthology to explore in a little detail what these seven words might mean in our understanding of prayer as the language of love. But love does not necessarily express itself in words. Words matter – but so does silence; so do the quiet courtesies of daily living; so do application, time out, effort, fun, sharing, self-giving. Love brings us into relationships with one another; and so it is with prayer. But prayer – like love in any relationship – has to cope with the routine and not merely with the peaks and troughs of our experience. 'It is in the grit of earth that we find the glory of heaven.'[23]

It will be noted that this is an anthology *for* prayer. It is not an anthology *of* prayer. In most cases, the quotations have been grouped together in broad categories around a common theme which might illuminate the seven key aspects of prayer as the language of love. Their sole purpose is to provide a starting point for reflection and response. They are concerned to inform our understanding of prayer *and* to lead us into prayer. It is therefore hoped that this anthology might commend itself for use in many different circumstances in the course of our lives, and not least of all in Lent, or on a private retreat, or at times when we discover our need to pray and to move on in the life of prayer.

'Christian prayer involves in various ways our making repeated approaches to the meaning of life as Jesus lived it.'[24] Faith and discipleship and prayer and action cannot be disentangled from each other. Prayer is the language of discipleship. It is the language of love. But 'love flies, runs, leaps for joy; it is free and unrestrained. Love gives all for all.'[25] May it be that a renewed understanding of prayer as the language of love – with its moments of insight, its frustrations, its delights, its disappointments, its torments, its call to enter into life – may help to bridge the gap between the theory and the practice of prayer.

JOHN MOSES
Southwell
2007

The Language of Love

Awareness

Arise my love, my fair one, and come away.
Song of Songs 2.10b

It is exactly here – at the beginning – that the analogy of human love is so helpful. We never know where or how or why or when it will strike. R. S. Thomas, the Welsh priest-poet, gives us the picture of a man – just like any other man – who 'was drawn to his knees and for no reason he knew'.[1] It is this not-uncommonplace experience that serves to remind us that prayer is 'God's activity in us'.[2]

The first word, *Awareness*, speaks of moments of recognition, of perception, of new insight; but it has an unpredictable quality. We don't find it just because we go looking for it; but we will never find it unless we are open to the possibility. It brings into play a variety of responses; but it asks that we look at life – at least for the moment – in a new way, that we see the promise in another person, in a particular situation, even – dare we say it? – in ourselves. It is as though we are seeing something for the first time: not seeing something in its entirety, but seeing enough to arouse our curiosity, our sense of wonder. It is 'to see the world in a grain of sand, and a Heaven in a wild flower, [to] hold Infinity in the palm of [our] hand and Eternity in an hour'.[3]

If we are wise, we will be mindful of our capacity for self-deception. Fleeting glances exchanged across a crowded room can be woefully misleading. The unheeding collusion with all that is going on around us; the delight in novelty for novelty's own sake; the preoccupation with how it feels rather than what it means: all these give good reason to be on our guard.

It is not the least of our problems that we 'are so obsessed with *doing* that we have no time and imagination left for *being*'.[4] Our moments of *awareness* might take us by surprise in the midst of life's activity, but the process of taking stock, of making them our own, of weaving something new into the fabric of our lives demands time.

The first word, *Awareness*, requires, then, an openness to sight and sound, to all that is happening around us, to life's surprises. It is the recognition of someone or something that takes us beyond ourselves. It carries with it a sense – albeit unspoken – that things may not be the same again. But let there be no facile assumption that *awareness* derives only from things that the heart might desire; it is born no less of our encounter with pain, with torment, with all that we abhor. *Awareness* – considered as the first step in the life of prayer – deepens our understanding of all that God is doing in the world, and it asks that we look at the way we see ourselves and relate to others.

Awareness presupposes a willingness to explore, to let go, to enter the depths. It is 'to be drawn by delight'.[5] There must be no going back; and to do so would be to deny the truth of what we have seen; it would be to place on hold, to condemn to the margins, something that might be vital to our integrity – and our potential – as a human being. 'Once the soul awakens, the search begins and you can never go back.'[6]

GOD'S ACTIVITY IN US

The first lesson we have to learn about prayer is that it is God's activity in us.

Mary Clare[1]

For thirty years I went in search of God, and when at the end of that time I opened my eyes, I discovered that it was He who had been looking for me.

Bayezid Bistani[2]

I pray not only because I am seeking God, but because God is also seeking me.

Anonymous

God is always present and waiting to be discovered now, in the present moment, precisely where we are and in what we are doing.

Harry Williams[3]

Whether you understand it or not, God loves you, is present to you, lives in you, dwells in you, calls you, saves you.

Thomas Merton[4]

Once the soul awakens, the search begins and you can never go back.

John O'Donohue[5]

THE INWARD JOURNEY

Prayer, then, is about daring to make the inward journey.

Michael Mayne[1]

The best journey to make
is inward. It is the interior
that calls.

R. S. Thomas[2]

Not anguish, not doubt, not a simple delight or joy, but hunger for reality takes hold of men and women driven to ponder on the nature of their lives and impels them to use prayer to penetrate below and beyond the appearances of things.

Alan Ecclestone[3]

Prayer arises from the depths of ourselves.

Renée Voillaume[4]

To be human is to pray.

Wendy Beckett[5]

We are what we pray.

Basil Hume[6]

DRAWN BY DELIGHT

Thoughts are our inner senses. Infused with silence and solitude, they bring out the mystery of the inner landscape.

John O'Donohue[1]

Here and there does not matter
We must be still and still moving
Into another intensity
For a further union, a deeper communion.

T. S. Eliot[2]

This above all else is needful: you must lay claim to nothing! Let go of yourself and let God act with you and in you as He will. This work is His, this word is His, this birth is His, in fact every single thing that you are.

Meister Eckhart[3]

The Holy Spirit is the wild and passionate side of God, the tactile spirit whose touch is around you, bringing you close to yourself and to others.

John O'Donohue[4]

What does it mean to be drawn by delight? 'Take delight in the Lord and He will give you the desires of your heart.'

Show me a lover and he will understand what I am saying. Show me someone who wants something, someone hungry, someone wandering in this wilderness, thirsting and longing

for the fountains of his eternal home, show me such a one and
he will know what I am meaning.

Augustine of Hippo[5]

Jerusalem . . . For me, it's as if there's a scent in the air, and
you pause for a second to sniff it, and something happens
inside you, and you begin to feel its pull – the scent of a love
not yet fully experienced, and of a truth not yet fully understood, and of a beauty not yet fully revealed.

John Hare[6]

I think that maybe
I will be a little surer
of being a little nearer.
That's all. Eternity
is in the understanding
that that little is more than enough.

R. S. Thomas[7]

ONE LIFE IN GOD

The children of God should not have any other country here below but the universe itself . . . That is the native city to which we owe our love.

Simone Weil[1]

We are all one life in God.

Jan van Ruysbroeck[2]

To see the world in a grain of sand
    And a Heaven in a wild flower,
Hold infinity in the palm of your hand
And eternity in an hour.

William Blake[3]

People may see the clouds chasing along, feel the wind, and notice the fish playing in the water. Yet they may not see, feel, and notice because they are not amazed by it.

Dorothee Soelle[4]

The world is deep, and deeper than the day could read. Deep is its woe. Joy deeper still than grief can be. Woe says: Hence, go! But joys want all eternity, want deep, profound eternity.

Friedrich Nietzsche[5]

STRETCHING HEARTS WIDE OPEN

Any teaching that sincerely fosters love of God and love of our neighbour for His sake, whatever life of religious observance or practice it may lead to, is more acceptable to God. For that is the love on account of which everything should come into being or cease to be, should be changed or left unchanged. That love is the source of all things and the final end towards which everything should be fittingly directed. Nor can anything be blameworthy that is done in truth on account of that love and in accordance with it.

Isaac of Stella[1]

Just as what brings heat makes things expand, so it is the gift of love to stretch hearts wide open.

John Chrysostom[2]

Prayer is the responsibility to meet others with all that I have, to be ready to encounter the unconditional in the conditional, to expect to meet God in the way, not to turn aside from the way.

John Robinson[3]

Ubi caritas et amor,
 Deus ibi est.
Congregavit nos in unum Christi amor.
Exsultemus et in ipso iucundemur
Timeamus et amemus Deum vivum.
Et ex corde diligamus nos sincero.
Ubi caritas et amor,
Deus ibi est.

Where charity and love are found,
There is God.
The love of Christ has gathered us together into one.
Let us rejoice and be glad in him.
Let us fear and love the living God,
And love each other from the depths of our heart.
Where charity and love are,
There is God.

Anonymous[4]

THE LANGUAGE OF LOVE

Prayer is a language of love; whenever it is not prayer is dispensable.

Dorothee Soelle[1]

A life of prayer then is a life of love.

Richard Benson[2]

Everybody loves; the question is, What do we love? Consequently we are not told not to love, but to choose what to love. But how can we choose, unless we are first chosen? We cannot love unless we are first loved.

Augustine of Hippo[3]

If you love, then follow. I do love, you say, but what way am I to follow . . . 'I am the way'.

Augustine of Hippo[4]

Love is absolutely vital for a human life. For love alone can awaken what is divine within you. In love, you grow and come home to your self.

John O'Donohue[5]

When love awakens in your life, it is like a rebirth, a new beginning.

John O'Donohue[6]

Men and women have changed their reasons for praying, their methods of prayer, their styles of life, but their need to pray has remained and grown throughout. Our task is to find what love means in the moment that lies before us now.

Alan Ecclestone[7]

Our ability to love is our ability to pray.

Basil Hume[8]

START WHERE YOU ARE

Prayer promises nothing but the staying with God. For far too long the Christian world has lived at ease with its faith, assumed too lightly that it knew how to pray, and dealt too carelessly with the stuff out of which prayer is to be made. There are dark days ahead.

Alan Ecclestone[1]

I cannot pray, therefore I come to pray.

Austin Farrer[2]

When a great moment knocks on the door of your life, it is often no louder than the beating of your heart, and it is very easy to miss it.

Boris Pasternak[3]

Prayer is the most personal of all activities, and it is therefore different for every person . . . What matters is that we come in the truth of our being.

Maria Boulding[4]

We must learn to pray as we are, and accept ourselves as we are, and not as the ideal people we would like to imagine ourselves to be.

Mary Clare[5]

The one thing that matters is that we always say Yes to God whenever we experience him.

Julian of Norwich[6]

If we want to pray, then we shall pray. There is nothing whatever that can hold us back.

Wendy Beckett[7]

In prayer we discover what we already have. You start where you are and deepen what you already have, and you realise that you are already there. We already have everything, but we don't know it and we don't experience it. Everything has been given to us in Christ. All we need is to experience what we already possess.

Thomas Merton[8]

Exploration

Let me see your face, let me hear your voice.
Song of Songs 2.14

If our moments of awareness provide hints of who God is, and how God works, and what God might ask of us, then *exploration* is about questioning, searching, testing. It is a time for pushing at the boundaries of our understanding. It carries the promise of a deeper intimacy, but that cannot be rushed. The questions that lovers might ask of themselves are no less pertinent here as we wrestle with the meaning of what we have found. What are the things that matter? Is there firm ground on which to stand? Do we have an appetite for each other?

Exploration presupposes a desire to move forward but there is no one pattern that is universally applicable. We stand at different points of entry, at different stages of development. What is necessary is the pattern, the pace, the rhythm that are right for us; remembering that 'each one of us has to learn to change step on occasion and alter the pace when some change comes round. Do it too often and you begin to stumble and fall. Fail to change step when needed and you run out of breath and stop.'[1]

Augustine of Hippo reminds us that, 'We do not come to God by navigation but by love';[2] and it is precisely here – as we feel our way – that we can all too easily lose our foothold. 'Too much of human life, including prayer, remains arrested at an adolescent stage.'[3] Evasion, fantasy, unreality have a way of taking over. The eye of love sees the possibilities in other human beings, in ordinary situations, but it does so in an honest and hard-headed way. There is no place for self-deception, for wishful thinking, for make-believe. Prayer cannot take place unless we are honest with God and with ourselves. 'Cheating is impossible.'[4]

Those who are concerned to grow in the life of prayer will remember that theology is the Church's primary discipline. It is our theology – complex, tentative, rudimentary, sophisticated, mature, critical, questioning as the case may be – that provides the backcloth against which our journey of *exploration* takes place. Our understanding of God, of ourselves, of other people, of God's purposes, of God's pattern of redemption will give definition to the perspectives that inform and colour our prayer.

In the Christian tradition – in the East and the West – the Bible has been 'the ground of true prayer'.[5] Lovers exchange familiar and oft-repeated words; and the scriptures provide all that we need as we explore prayer as the language of love. But words – our words – can become self-conscious, intrusive. They can trip us up.

> I have been a student of your love
> and have not graduated. Setting
> my own questions, I bungled
> the examination: Where? When? Why? [6]

Let it not be forgotten that 'God's voice speaks most often in silence'.[7] The *exploration* of prayer – like the exploration of lovers – demands space, solitude, simplicity. 'True silence is the speech of lovers.'[8]

It is part of the grace of silence that we learn to receive. *Exploration* is a two-way street. In the language of love, there is giving and receiving. We dare not live as though we are only accountable to ourselves. There are signposts and boundary markers along the way – for guidance, for protection, and for the well-being of all interested parties. Students of prayer must learn one of the early lessons of loving: that, 'My freedom is not fully free when left to itself. It becomes so when it is brought into the right relation with the freedom of another.'[9]

But do not let the analogy of human love, of erotic love, suggest that prayer is merely personal piety – enclosed, self-authenticating. It is part of the work of *exploration* to discover something of the extent to which we are all bound up in one another. 'Our prayer is public and for all, and when we pray, we pray not for a single person, but for the whole people, because we are all one.'[10]

[19]

UNREALITY AND DREAMS

How can you pray?
It is nearly impossible to pray, but the overcoming of that impossibility, that is just what prayer is.

Austin Farrer[1]

Each man or woman who prays is at such a different stage of development and there are so many ways of entry – and of evasion.

Thomas Merton[2]

We live in a world of unreality and dreams. To give up our imaginary position as the centre, to renounce it, not only intellectually but in the imaginative part of our soul, that means to awaken to what is real and eternal, to see the true light and hear the true silence.

Simone Weil[3]

If we really want to pray, we'll have to give it time. We must slow down to a human tempo and we'll begin to have time to listen. And as soon as we listen to what's going on, things will begin to take shape by themselves. But for this we have to experience time in a new way.

Thomas Merton[4]

To pray is to make the most of our moments of perception.

Alan Ecclestone[5]

FINDING OUR WAY

Prayer is an encounter and a relationship.

Anthony Bloom[1]

My freedom is not fully free when left to itself. It becomes so when it is brought into the right relation with another.

Thomas Merton[2]

Lord, I am tired. I can bring to thee
Only a heavy weight of tiredness.
I kneel, but all my mind's a vacancy
And conscious only of its weariness –
Can it be prayer, this dragging dreariness?

'The effectual fervent prayer avails',
Wrote downright James; and here inert kneel I;
I would feel fervent but the effort fails;
Like some starved mendicant, too weak to cry
His need. I wait – perchance Thou wilt pass by.

Andrew[3]

The life of prayer is not a journey in which we note successive milestones passed, but one in which we set out once again from our departure point, going up with gladness to the holy city or going down sick at heart, as the case may be, with greater knowledge of the joy and pain involved.

Alan Ecclestone[4]

Too much of human life, including prayer, remains arrested at an adolescent stage.

Alan Ecclestone[5]

The point is that each of us has to find for himself the rhythmical pace at which he can keep going in his prayers, each of us has to learn to change step on occasion and alter the pace when the time for some change comes round. Do it too often and you begin to stumble and falter. Fail to change step when needed and you run out of breath and stop. Much of praying consists in saying old words in a way that makes them new, in refusing to let them go dead by treating them as if they were not able to be new words. This is not a mechanical view of praying but in truth its opposite, taking note of our make-up, age, condition of body and mind.

Alan Ecclestone[6]

Prayer is its own end and not a means to obtain a particular goal.

Dorothee Soelle[7]

OUR DEEPEST FREEDOM

Our encounter with God should be . . . the discovery of our own deepest freedom.

Thomas Merton[1]

Prayer is the truest guarantee of personal freedom.

Thomas Merton[2]

Being called is also letting oneself be called.

Dorothee Soelle[3]

All prayer demands that we look at God . . . and do what seems to work.

Wendy Beckett[4]

Prayer seeks to break new ground. Prayer wants a world made new. Prayer tries to find its own authentic voice.

Alan Ecclestone[5]

When [God] leaves the choice to us, then of course we must strive to follow Him step by step as exactly as possible, to share His life as He lived it . . . Love compels us to this imitation. If God leaves us this choice, this freedom, it is precisely because He wants us to spread our sails to the wind of pure love and, impelled by Him, to hasten after Him in the sweet scent of His fragrance, in an exact imitation.

Charles de Foucauld[6]

Only the person who seeks everything in God prays to Him . . . Only the person who seeks nothing in himself seeks everything in God.

Karl Barth[7]

THE SIMPLEST WAY

The real difficulty about prayer is that it has no difficulty.

Wendy Beckett[1]

If you want a life of prayer, the way to get it is by praying.

Thomas Merton[2]

Prayer is most truly prayer when it is uttered in the simplest way.

Alan Ecclestone[3]

God works most in a humble heart, for He has greatest opportunity to work therein, and finds His most like therein.

Meister Eckhart[4]

What will God deny to a prayer which proceeds from spirit and truth, seeing it is He who demands it?

Tertullian[5]

If you desire to gain what you do not enjoy,
you must go where you enjoy nothing;

if you desire to reach what you do not know,
you must go where you know nothing;

if you desire to reach what you do not possess,
you must go where you possess nothing;

if you desire to become what you are not,
you must go where you are nothing.

John of the Cross[6]

SUPERFLUOUS WORDS

Away with much use of words in prayer, yes; but let there
be intensive prayer if fervent concentration persists. Saying much when we pray means doing a necessary thing with
superfluous words.

Augustine of Hippo[1]

We need words to help us recollect ourselves and see what
we are asking for; not to make us suppose that the
Lord must be given information or swayed by words.

Augustine of Hippo[2]

You do not go to God with a platform for speeches or an
agenda for discussion. It simply is not possible to channel
a conversation with God the way you would like. God goes off
at a tangent. He corners you by bringing out into the open the
real questions which you have been studiously avoiding.

Then God turns the tables on you. Now he asks the questions and you have to provide the answer.

Alessandro Pronzato[3]

THE SILENT LANGUAGE OF LOVE

God's voice speaks most often in silence.
He who cannot keep silence is not contented with God.

Herbert Kelly[1]

God is the friend of silence.

Teresa of Calcutta[2]

I cannot get Galilee out of my head. To think he remained silent for thirty years. Such a silence.

Jean Sullivan[3]

That which we most need in order to make progress is to be silent before God . . . for the language that He best hears is the silent language of love.

John of the Cross[4]

True silence is the speech of lovers. For only love knows its beauty, completeness and utter joy. True silence is a garden enclosed, where alone the soul can meet its God. It is a sealed fountain that He alone can unseal to slacken the soul's infinite thirst for him.

Catherine de Hueck Doherty[5]

Sometimes the most important thresholds of mystery are places of silence.

John O'Donohue[6]

ONE IN GOD

He is – and this reality absorbs everything else.

Thomas Merton[1]

Discovering God in ourselves and in all things means sensing the presence of mystery everywhere, mystery which evokes wonder, love, awe, tenderness, terror, interest, fascination – mystery.

Harry Williams[2]

The discovery of ourselves in God, and of God in ourselves, by a charity that also finds all other people in God with ourselves is, therefore, not a discovery of ourselves but of Christ.

Thomas Merton[3]

Our prayer is public and for all, and when we pray, we pray not for a single person, but for the whole people, because we are all one.

Cyprian[4]

In our dealings with God, He is free and so are we. It's simply a need for me to express my love by praying for my friends; it's like embracing them. If you love another person, it's God's love being realised. One and the same love is reaching your friend through you, and you through your friend.

Thomas Merton[5]

Prayer the Churches banquet. Angels age,
  God's breath in man returning to his birth,
   The soul in paraphrase, heart in pilgrimage,
The Christian plummet sounding heav'n and earth;
Engine against th'Almightie, sinners towre,
   Reversed thunder, Christ-side-piercing spear,
   The six-daies world transposing in an houre,
A kinde of time, which all things heare and feare;
Softness, and peace, and joy, and love, and blisse,
   Exalted Manna, gladnesse of the best,
   Heaven in ordinarie, man well drest,
The milkie way, the bird of Paradise,
   Church-bels beyond the starres heard, the souls blood,
   The land of spices; something understood.

George Herbert[6]

We are to pray . . . as those who join in the dawn-chorus
of a new creation.

Alan Ecclestone[7]

Passion

Let my beloved come to his garden, and eat its choicest fruits.
Song of Songs 4.16b

'Love is not amiable complacency. Love is fire.'[1] Awareness, exploration – yes, of course; but there comes a point in the passage of true love when desire gives way to *passion*. The prayer of the consecrated life – 'I want to give God everything'[2] – echoes the self-giving, the self-abandonment, of lovers. *Passion* is uninhibited, unconstrained. It tells of being lost and found, of letting go, of handing over. It speaks of total delight.

There is an immediacy, an intensity, an urgency about the *passion* of love. 'My God and my love. You are all mine and I am yours.'[3] The words hint at more than most of us are able to give, but there are fleeting moments – fleeting but potentially decisive moments – when 'love gives all for all'.[4] We cannot live at that pitch. The ecstasy of love will always be tempered and weathered by routine. It is the love that 'bears all things, believes all things, hopes all things, endures all things'[5] that remains.

Passion – the passion that properly belongs to prayer as the language of love – might therefore appear to be self-contained, self-indulgent. The truth is the very opposite. It is prayer without passion – as surely as it is lives without passion – that can so easily become sterile, restricted, self-absorbed. *Passion* – because it does not compete, compel or constrain – becomes the integrating factor: making connections, drawing the disparate parts of our world and of our personalities into some kind of order, giving shape and focus and priority. '*Because* God is all that matters, *therefore* everything else at last begins to matter as it should.'[6]

Perhaps I betray my own convictions about God and life and Christian discipleship when I say that the *passion* of prayer is about life and love and laughter and joy and self-giving. But there is pain. Prayer is always *in* God. It is never merely something that is addressed *to* God. And 'the very life of God by which we live is an everlasting giving of Himself away'.[7] That is why it is helpful to think of prayer as a vast energy field in which unexpected connections are made, lives are transformed, and new things become possible.

'A prayer makes sense only if it is lived.'[8] Alan Ecclestone's critique of engagement without passion and of passion without engagement is uncomfortably apposite. The former is described as 'a heartless hoax, a mere formality'; the latter is dismissed as 'a display of fireworks, a waste of energy, a self-abuse'.[9] Writings about prayer – the theory and the practice – are all too easily littered with large-sounding words. The heart of the matter is expressed very simply: 'All that I can do is reduced to one word only, and that is love.'[10] It is therefore the connection – the open dialogue, the working relationship – between passion and action that must be established and sustained. There is an empathy of prayer which we enter secretly, silently. There is an activity of prayer which we enter with forethought and resolution. Both are born of that passionate engagement with God in prayer and in life which we find in Jesus.

A LIVING FLAME

Love is watchful, and while resting, never sleeps; weary, it is never exhausted; imprisoned, it is never in bonds; alarmed, it is never afraid; like a living flame and a burning torch, it surges upward and surely surmounts every obstacle. Whoever loves God knows well the sound of His voice. A loud cry in the ears of God is that burning love of the soul which exclaims, 'My God and my love, You are all mine, and I am Yours'.

Thomas à Kempis[1]

This above all else is needful; you must lay claim to nothing! Let go of yourself and let God act with you and in you as He will . . . Be as a desert in respect of yourself and all things.

Meister Eckhart[2]

Thank you, Lord, thank you!
    Why me, why did you choose me?
Joy, joy, tears of joy.

Michel Quoist[3]

Lord, I love you, and I want to love you more.
    It's you who make love eternal, and I want to love eternally.

Michel Quoist[4]

I want to give God everything.

Thomas Merton[5]

A FIRE EVER BURNING

O eternal Trinity, God, you are an abyss, a deep sea; you have given yourself to me – what greater could you give? You are a fire, ever burning but never consumed, consuming in your heart all the self-love of the soul, taking away all coldness.

Catherine of Siena[1]

G od never gives, nor did He ever give a gift, merely that [we] might have it and be content with it. No, all gifts which He ever gave in heaven or on earth, He gave with one sole purpose – to make one single gift: Himself. With all His gifts He desires only to prepare us for the one gift, which is Himself.

Meister Eckhart[2]

L ate have I loved you, O Beauty so ancient and so new; late have I loved you! For behold you were within me, and I outside; and I sought you outside and in my ugliness fell upon those lovely things that you have made. You were with me and I was not with you. I was kept from you by those things, yet had they not been in you, they would not have been at all. You called and cried to me and broke open my deafness: and you sent forth your beams and shone upon me and chased away my blindness: you breathed fragrance upon me, and I drew in my breath and do now pant for you: I tasted you, and now hunger and thirst for you; you touched me, and I have burned for your peace.

Augustine of Hippo[3]

TOTAL LOVE: TOTAL TRUTH

All that I aim to do is reduced to one word only, and that is, love.

Thomas Ken[1]

Love is not consolation. It is light.

Simone Weil[2]

I can see God's love only when I become part of it myself.

Dorothee Soelle[3]

Total love sees us in total truth because it is only He who sees us totally.

Wendy Beckett[4]

Wholeness comes about by letting Him pull our wholeness into being during prayer.

Wendy Beckett[5]

All you can do is to be at every single moment as true as you can with all the power in your being – and then leave it to God to use you, even despite yourself.

Anthony Bloom[6]

The passion of God that arises from prayer . . . is never a narrowing passion. It does not drive out our other desires, but integrates them and makes them absolute in their truth. *Because* God is all that matters, *therefore* everything else at last begins to matter as it should.

Wendy Beckett[7]

SINGING THE SONG OF LOVE

Love flies, runs, leaps for joy; it is free and unrestrained. Love gives all for all, resting in One who is highest above all things, from whom every good flows and proceeds. Love does not regard the gifts, but turns to the Giver of all good gifts. Love knows no limits, but ardently transcends all bounds. Love feels no burden, takes no account of toil, attempts things beyond its strength; love sees nothing as impossible, for it feels able to achieve all things. Love therefore does great things; it is strong and effective; while he who lacks love faints and fails.

Thomas à Kempis[1]

We enter God's energy when we pray.

Wendy Beckett[2]

Prayer is above all a tremendous act of hope . . . It is God's business: we surrender in trust to Him.

Wendy Beckett[3]

When you begin to let go, it is amazing how rich your life becomes . . . Then what is real, what you love deeply, what really belongs to you, comes deeper into you.

John O'Donohue[4]

Before I am lost-and-found in God's love I should like to make one thing more, a song or half-song or no song, but one thing more in thanksgiving for having seen and known and lived and died.

Christopher Fry[5]

Let me sing the song of love.

Thomas à Kempis[6]

PLUMBING NEW DEPTHS

You never enjoy the world aright till the sea itself floweth in your veins, till you are clothed with the heavens, and crowned with the stars; and perceive yourself to be the sole heir of the whole world, and more than so, because men and women are in it who are sole heirs as well as you. Till you can sing and rejoice and delight in God, as misers do in gold, and kings in sceptres, you never enjoy the world.

Thomas Traherne[1]

Passion must plumb new depths, and men and women must pray to affirm their faith in the Hidden God, in God who has taken manhood in to Himself, in God whose Son's Passion proclaims for ever the mystery of existence. Men and women must pray because only so can they learn to live and grow to their true stature in a world like this which will for ever disclose more questions than answers, in which their freedom will for ever be the trial of their faith, in which the dimensions of moral and mental pain take on quite new proportions.

Alan Ecclestone[2]

In the kingdom of love there is no competition; there is no possessiveness or control. The more love you give away, the more love you will have.

John O'Donohue[3]

Prayer is God's taking possession of me ... We are only asked to allow Him to take possession.

Wendy Beckett[4]

[36]

The authenticity of love must imply a totality of giving.

W. H. Vanstone[5]

Love is *self*-giving.

W. H. Vanstone[6]

The human journey is a continuous act of transfiguration.

John O'Donohue[7]

THE DOOR OF THE KINGDOM

Find the door of your heart, you will discover it is the door of the Kingdom of God.

John Chrysostom[1]

Where love is, action is destined to pass into passion.

W. H. Vanstone[2]

Whoever loves much, does much.

Thomas à Kempis[3]

A prayer makes sense only if it is lived.

Anthony Bloom[4]

Engagement without passion is a heartless hoax, a mere formality that one day shows itself to have been no engagement at all, for there is no real engagement of ourselves with others that is not costly.

Passion without engagement is a display of fireworks, a waste of energy, a self-abuse, 'full of sound and fury, signifying nothing'. It burns itself out to leave only ashes. Its intensity can scorch and scar but not transfigure. It knows and offers no guide to the worth of what it touches.

Alan Ecclestone[5]

LOVE'S ENERGY WORKING LOVE

Love is the threshold where divine and human presence ebb and flow into each other.

John O'Donohue[1]

Love acts of its own initiative, under no compulsion or constraint, in order that another may benefit; and the activity which is characteristic of love is, in principle, without limit or qualification.

W. H. Vanstone[2]

Happy are we if we put into practice what we hear and sing. For our hearing is a sowing of seed and our actions the fruit of that seed.

Augustine of Hippo[3]

Only in prayer can God draw us into a fiery commitment that is never fanatical.

Wendy Beckett[4]

We pray, Lord, that everything we do may be prompted by your inspiration, so that every prayer and work of ours may begin from you and be brought by you to completion.

Benedict of Nursia[5]

Heaven's not a place . . .
No! it's a dance
Where love perpetual,
Rhythmical, musical,
Maketh advance
Loved one to Lover.

R. S. Thomas[6]

The earth is filled with the Spirit of God,
  Creative, powerful, free,
Encounter as wind unseen.

Sweep through our hearts and renew us in God,
Life-giving breath from on high,
Love's energy working love.

Sing to His glory, fling wide His praise,
People redeemed and set free,
Caught in the shout of heaven's joy.

Office Hymn, West Malling[7]

Pain

I sought him whom my soul loves;
I sought him, but found him not;
I called him, but he gave no answer.
Song of Songs 3.1

Passion and *pain* can never be entirely disentangled. It is true for those who love. It is true for those who pray. If prayer is 'the search for a relationship',[1] then we ought not to be surprised if we find that we are tested. That is how relationships are! And the more intimate – the more committed – the relationship, the more searching, the more testing, it will be.

This is not to confuse the *pain* of prayer with the frustrations, the betrayals, the breakdowns of everyday relationships, but it is to acknowledge that prayer so often comes out of the poverty and the emptiness in which we stand. 'Those parts of our own individual existence that seem least pious or "together" may be the points at which we are exposed to God, and so the points from which we most truly come to live in Christ.'[2] It was the tax collector – and not the Pharisee – who went down to his house justified.[3]

Lovers who have been tested by the traumas of ordinary relationships are able to testify that brokenness can be the seedbed of new life. *Pain* can therefore be seen as an unavoidable – indeed, a necessary – aspect of prayer as the language of love if there is to be growth.

The *pain* of prayer will be experienced in a variety of ways. There is the absence – or the perceived absence – of God, 'the empty silence within'.[4] These are the times when what we *feel* can no longer sustain us; but those who have stayed the course will know that 'the day when God is absent, when He is silent – that is the beginning of prayer'.[5]

There is the tortured relationship: What difference does it make? What does it mean? Is it really working? Is this all there is? It is a commonplace experience for lovers *and* for those who pray or try to pray. Prayer can be 'so sweet that people go to it as to a dance', but it can also be 'so difficult that people go to it as if it were a battle'.[6] And yet there is the salutary reminder that 'the prayer of question and accusation and even hostility to God is genuine prayer . . . It is true that we are nearest to

God when we are loving Him but we are certainly very close when we are fighting Him.'[7]

But there is also the *pain* that is far more conspicuously a consequence of prayer as a language of love. Passion and pain cannot be disentangled from each other in either the empathy or the activity of prayer. Empathy requires a quiet and unselfconscious sharing in the pain of the world: in solitude, in silent offering, in fasting, in intercession. It comes out of the recognition that 'when we pray we are inextricably bound up with the answer'.[8] Activity requires nothing less, even though the context might be public and the response vocal, practical. In both instances – empathy and activity – it is passion *and* engagement that are required, because 'those who pray search not only in their own hearts but they plunge deep into the heart of the whole world in order to listen more intently to the deepest and most neglected voices that proceed from its inner depths'.[9]

What is challenged here is the facile assumption that prayer is nothing more than a pious refuge. If passion speaks of self-giving, *pain* reminds us of the cost of 'a continually renewed and continually deepening relationship with God'.[10] Prayer has its patterns, its disciplines; but *pain* speaks above all of the love – tested and bruised though it might be – which enables us to stay with the possibility of a rich harvest even as the seed is buried in the ground.

THAT GREAT ABSENCE

Why no! I never thought other than
    That God is that great absence
In our lives, the empty silence
Within, the place where we go
Seeking, not in hope to
Arrive or find. He keeps the interstices
In our knowledge, the darkness
Between stars. His are the echoes
We follow, the footprints he has just
Left. We put our hands in
His side hoping to find
It warm. We look at people
And places as though he had looked
At them, too; but miss the reflection.

R. S. Thomas[1]

The day when God is absent, when He is silent – that is the beginning of prayer.

Anthony Bloom[2]

EVEN WHEN IT IS NIGHT

He is that great void
we must enter, calling
to one another on our way
in the direction from which
he blows. What matter
if we should never arrive
to breed or to winter
in the climate of our conception?

Enough we have been given wings
and a needle in the mind
to respond to his bleak north.
There are times even at the Pole
when he, too, pauses in his withdrawal,
so that it is light there all night long.

R. S. Thomas[1]

That eternal Spring lies hidden.
How well I know its hiding place,
Even when it is night.

In the dark night of this life
How well I know in faith the sacred spring,
Even when it is night.

I do not know its source, for it has none,
But I know that every source comes from it,
Even when it is night.

John of the Cross[2]

LIVING A DYING LIFE

God can make prayer so sweet that people go to it as to a dance; and God can make prayer so difficult that people go to it as if it were a battle.

Nicholas of Flue[1]

There can be no serious practice of prayer which is not accompanied by darkness and a sense of unreality.

Basil Hume[2]

Prayer if it is real is an acknowledgement of our finitude, our need, our openness to be changed, our readiness to be surprised, yes astonished by the 'beams of love'.

Thomas Merton[3]

Prayer requires our personal co-operation and response to the Spirit . . . Each person must decide whether he or she is willing to pay the cost of entering into a continually renewed and continually deepening relationship with God in prayer.

Mary Clare[4]

Be assured of this, that we must live a dying life. And the more completely we die to self, the more we begin to live to God.

Thomas à Kempis[5]

THE ESSENTIAL HEART OF PRAYER

There is a long tradition of prayer as argument with God. The prayer of question and accusation and even hostility to God is genuine prayer . . . It is true that we are nearest to God when we are loving him, but we are certainly very close when we are fighting him.

J. Neville Ward[1]

We must relate prayer to conversion of life. Prayer, which is the fruit of true conversion, is an activity, an adventure, and sometimes a dangerous one, since there are occasions when it brings neither peace nor comfort, but challenge, conflict and new responsibility. This is why so many old ways of praying, and books about prayer, seem to have let us down. Too often when we used them we were hoping to get something for ourselves from prayer, perhaps security or a growing sensible realisation and knowledge of God. To seek such things in prayer is a mistake. The essential heart of prayer is the throwing away of ourselves in self-oblation to God, so that He can do with us what He wills. Any form of prayer which does not incite a costly giving in love soon becomes sterile, dry and a formal duty. Prayer is thus the search for a relationship.

Mary Clare[2]

Prayer seeks to see where the mortice and tenon, the dovetailing of eternal and temporal things, has come awry, and how re-engagement in penitence and hope may be made.

Alan Ecclestone[3]

DEEP INTO THE HEART OF THE WORLD

This age which by its very nature is a time of crisis . . . calls for the special searching and questioning which is the work of the Christian in silence . . . for those who pray search not only in their own hearts but they plunge deep into the heart of the whole world in order to listen more intently to the deepest and most neglected voices that proceed from its inner depths.

Thomas Merton[1]

To bring the world before God in prayer is to stand where you can hear most clearly the most tragic voice in the universe, God's despair of man, 'Whom shall I send and who will go for us?'

J. Neville Ward[2]

[Nothing in prayer is concerned to liberate us from] the ordinary struggles and sufferings of human existence . . . And for that very reason the dimensions of prayer in solitude are those of our ordinary anguish, our self-searching, our moments of nausea at our own vanity, falsity, and capacity for betrayal.

Thomas Merton[3]

Christian hope sends us back to our life on earth in a wholly new way . . . The Christian does not need a last refuge in the eternal from earthly tasks and difficulties. But like Christ Himself, we must drink the earthly cup to the lees and only in our doing that is the crucified and risen Lord with us and we, crucified and risen with Christ. This world must not be prematurely written off . . . Christ takes hold of us in the centre of our life.

Dietrich Bonhoeffer[4]

A Christianity that is free of suffering leaves suffering to others.

Dorothee Soelle[5]

S uffering for the neighbour grows the more as the soul unites itself through love with God.

John of the Cross[6]

WATCHING WITH CHRIST

Silence is passionate.

Wendy Beckett[1]

Each time you take a human soul with you into prayer, you accept from God a piece of spiritual work with all its implications and with all its cost – a cost which may mean for you spiritual exhaustion and darkness, and may even include vicarious suffering, the Cross.

Evelyn Underhill[2]

. . . how to cope
with trampled hearts,
crushed souls,
victims of spiritual banditry.

The best thing
is to say nothing
but merely
suffer with them.

Don Helder Camara[3]

[Christianity means] living unreservedly in life's duties, problems, successes and failures, experiences and perplexities. In doing so we throw ourselves completely into the arms of God, taking seriously, not our own sufferings, but those of God in the world – watching with Christ in Gethsemane.

Dietrich Bonhoeffer[4]

Every Christian prayer for others involves the realisation that we who pray are inextricably bound up with the answer. Our prayer is not a mere message sent to God, voicing a request. It carries us with it deep into all that costly action which is the purpose of God in the life of the world.

J. Neville Ward[5]

Suffering does not necessarily separate us from God. It may actually put us in touch with the mystery of reality. To follow Christ means to take part in His life.

Dorothee Soelle[6]

SIT DOWN AND TASTE MY MEAT

Lord you seized me and I could not resist you.
I ran for a long time, but you followed me.
I took by-paths but you knew them.

You overtook me.
I struggled.
You won.

Here I am Lord, out of breath, no fight left in me, and I've
said 'yes' almost unwillingly.
When I stood there trembling like one defeated before his
captor,
Your look of love fell on me.

Michel Quoist[1]

Love bade me welcome: yet my soul drew back,
    Guiltie of dust and sinne.
But quick-ey'd Love, observing me grow slack
    From my first entrance in,
Drew nearer to me, sweetly questioning,
    If I lacked anything.

A guest, I answer'd, worthy to be here:
    Love said, You shall be he.
I, the unkinde, ungratefull? Ah my deare,
    I cannot look on Thee.
Love took my hand, and smiling did reply,
    Who made the eyes but I?

Truth Lord, but I have marr'd them: let my shame
    Go where it doth deserve.
And know you not, sayes Love, who bore the blame?
    My deare, then I will serve.
You must sit down, sayes Love, and taste my meat:
So I did sit and eat.

George Herbert[2]

Patience

Whither has your beloved gone . . . Whither has your beloved
turned, that we may seek him with you.

Song of Songs 6.1

Patience is one of the key building blocks in any relationship. If it is love that enables us to stay with the pain, the virtue – the grace – that is required is *patience*. Just as in marriage there are times when it is the will to make the marriage work that makes all the difference, so it is in the life of prayer. It is the growth that is willed, desired, worked at, that is so important. *Patience* is, therefore, something much more than a disciplined perseverance. It is better understood as 'the concentration, the effort, the unsparingness of self-giving that are involved in love'.[1]

Prayer – like love – has its many facets, its changing moods.

You must remain
kneeling. Even as this moon
making its way through the earth's
cumbersome shadow, prayer, too
has its phases.[2]

Patience, which is one of prayer's inescapable phases, speaks then of our willingness to be still, to watch, to wait. It is true in all relationships that 'love involves waiting';[3] and so it is in prayer – the language of love – that 'simply waiting for God in silence *is* prayer. Indeed it is the most profound form of prayer that men and women in their torn and suffering state can offer to God.'[4] But this vocation – to wait in the darkness : unseeing, unknowing – is not the cheerless, barren occupation it might appear to be. Those who have travelled this way tell of 'the absolute primacy and necessity of silent, hidden, poor, apparently fruitless prayer'.[5]

But waiting requires an appropriate degree of solitude. The ancient insight remains: 'We are what we do with our silence.'[6] Temperament, life-style, the legitimate demands and expectations of others may all militate against the solitude and the silence in which this waiting upon God can take place, but

– acknowledged or not – there is the need for us to find that 'inner hermitage in which to meet our God'.[7] It is here that the patience that love requires – in life and in prayer – can be nurtured. 'God is the friend of silence,'[8] and it is not the least of His gifts as we persevere in the solitude of silence that we learn to listen, to see, and to accept.

We learn to listen. The solitude of silence, albeit brief and punctuated by all sorts of preconceived ideas and images, can provide the space in which to listen and learn. There is always the temptation to impose ourselves upon the silence, to indulge in wishful thinking, to retreat into a fantasy world, to evade the truth that is there waiting to be claimed. It is only as we begin to listen to ourselves as well as to others that we understand the need 'to face myself exactly as I am, with all my limitations, and to accept others as they are, with all *their* limitations'.[9]

We learn to see. 'Prayer is not necessarily best described as always looking towards God; sometimes, and especially in intercession, it is equally a learning to look at the world as if with God's eyes.'[10] This is not easily achieved. The culture of church life does not encourage us to look upon God in silence; and no amount of looking will enable us to see with God's eyes if minds are not informed and hearts remain unmoved. It may be that 'by loving our neighbour we are given the sight of God',[11] but to turn doing into seeing and seeing into doing requires a rigour – patient and purposeful – which is most easily achieved by those whose lives are hid with Christ in God.[12]

We learn to accept. It is in the solitude and silence of prayer that many begin to find the truth about themselves and other people – and learn to live with it. We can find ourselves. 'Many people miss out on themselves as they journey through life. They know others, they know places, they know skills, they know their work, but tragically, they do not know themselves at all.'[13] We can find other people. There are many situations in which we need a good deal of patience if trust is to 'take root and grow'.[14] But just as in love men and women are able to find something of their own wholeness, so it is in prayer that we begin to understand, to accept and to trust. 'The whole thing boils down to giving ourselves in prayer a chance to realise that we have what we seek. We don't have to rush after it. It is there all the time, and if we give it time it will make itself known to us.'[15]

The tradition of waiting in silence can be the springboard for growth in prayer. 'We must accept that we will never know the meaning of prayer without perseverance in the act of praying itself.'[16] There will certainly be a need for direction, for counselling. We need to open our minds to the insights of others – books, wise friends, totally new ways of looking at things. 'Patience obtains all things';[17] and it is only by virtue of the hard slog – *patience* – that we learn to listen to the things we do not want to hear, to see the things to which our eyes have been closed, to accept the things we do not understand and would not choose if left to ourselves. But then – and perhaps only then – will we discover that 'our poor attempt to pray is never wasted'.[18]

THE INNER HERMITAGE

Not everyone can or should live as a hermit. But no Christian can do without an inner hermitage in which to meet his God.

A Monk[1]

Unless we can find God within ourselves, in the depth of our own solitude, we will never find him at all. It may be that until we have found and been transformed by Him there, we will not be able to attain to the vision which enables us to see Him in everything.

Anonymous[2]

Christians become conscious of their aloneness in the silence of prayer . . . In aloneness we learn to share in the emptiness and lostness of modern man.

Mary Clare[3]

Human solitude is so unsolitary. Deep human solitude is a place of great affinity and of tension. When you come into your solitude, you come into companionship with everything and everyone.

John O'Donohue[4]

A TIME OF WAITING

... the absolute primacy and necessity of silent, hidden, poor, apparently fruitless prayer.

Thomas Merton[1]

L ove involves waiting.

Clare[2]

S imply waiting for God in silence *is* prayer. Indeed, it is the most profound form of prayer that men and women in their torn and suffering state can offer to God.

Ladislaus Boros[3]

W aiting is not despair. It is the acceptance of our not having, in the power of that which we already have.

Paul Tillich[4]

O ur time is a time of waiting; waiting is its special destiny. And every time is a time of waiting, waiting for the breaking in of eternity. All time runs forward. All time, both in history and in personal life, is expectation. Time itself is waiting, waiting not for another time, but for that which is eternal.

Paul Tillich[5]

L et nothing disturb you.
Let nothing frighten you.
All things pass away:
God never changes.

Patience obtains all things.
They who find God
Find they lack nothing:
God alone suffices.

Teresa of Avila[6]

LOOKING AND LISTENING

Grey waters, vast
        as an area of prayer
that one enters. Daily
        over a period of years
I have let the eye rest on them.
Was I waiting for something?
                Nothing
but that continuous waving
        that is without meaning
occurred.
        Ah, but a rare bird is
rare. It is when one is not looking,
at times one is not there
                that it comes.
You must wear your eyes out,
as others their knees.
        I became the hermit
of the rocks, habited with the wind
and the mist. There were days,
so beautiful the emptiness
it might have filled,
                its absence
was as its presence; not to be told
any more, so single my mind
after its long fast,
        my watching from praying.

R. S. Thomas[1]

Prayer is not necessarily best described as always looking towards God; sometimes, and especially in intercession, it is equally a learning to look at the world as if with God's eyes.

Rowan Williams[2]

You do not yet see God, but by loving your neighbour you gain the sight of God; by loving your neighbour you purify your eye for seeing God.

Augustine of Hippo[3]

The first duty we owe to others is to listen to them.

It is the characteristic of God's love for us that He does not content Himself with speaking to us, but also listens to us.

To learn to listen to our brother or sister is therefore to do for them what God has done for us.

Dietrich Bonhoeffer[4]

TO PRAY TRUE

God is the friend of silence.

Teresa of Calcutta[1]

I gaze myself into accepting
that to pray true is to say nothing.

R. S. Thomas[2]

Many are avidly seeking, but they alone find who remain
in continual silence.

Isaac of Nineveh[3]

The most adequate prayer will be a silent prayer for when
we are silent we are one, when we speak we are two.

P. A. H. de Boer[4]

The Father uttered one Word: that Word is His Son, and He
utters Him for ever in everlasting silence; and in silence
the soul has to hear it.

John of the Cross[5]

Contemplation is essentially a listening in silence.

Thomas Merton[6]

We are what we do with our silence.

Origen[7]

THE COURAGE TO FACE MYSELF

Silence is the sister of the Divine.

John O'Donohue[1]

The discovery of Christ is never genuine if it is nothing but a flight from ourselves. On the contrary, it cannot be an escape. It must be a fulfilment. I cannot discover in myself and myself in Him unless I have the courage to face myself exactly as I am, with all my limitations, and to accept others as they are, with all *their* limitations. The religious answer is not religious if it is not fully real. Evasion is the answer of superstition.

Thomas Merton[2]

In the midst of prayer that is dry, desolate and repugnant, unconscious fantasies may take over.

Thomas Merton[3]

If we don't face our selfishness and recognise it in our prayers, it will be driven underground and appear only in disguise in something noble and good.

Harry Williams[4]

If you are selfish in your prayers there is not much hope that you will be really unselfish anywhere else.

William Temple[5]

Nothing is colder than a Christian who does not care for the salvation of others.

John Chrysostom[6]

Do not have Jesus Christ on your lips, and the world in your heart.

Ignatius of Antioch[7]

LET NOTHING HINDER ME

We must accept the fact that we shall never know the true meaning of prayer without perseverance in the act of praying itself.

Mary Clare[1]

The waves run up the shore
and fall back. I run
up the approaches of God
and fall back. The breakers return
reaching a little further,
gnawing away at the main land.
They have done this thousands
of years, exposing little by little
the rock under the soil's face.
I must imitate them only
in my return to the assault,
not in their violence. Dashing
my prayers at him will achieve
little other than the exposure
of the rock under his surface.
My returns must be made
on my knees. Let despair be known
as my ebb-tide; but let prayer
have its springs, too, brimming,
disarming him; discovering somewhere
among his fissures deposits of mercy
where trust may take root and grow.

R. S. Thomas[2]

The whole thing boils down to giving ourselves in prayer a chance to realise that we have what we seek. We don't have to rush after it. It is there all the time, and if we give it time it will make itself known to us.

Thomas Merton[3]

It pleases God that we should work away at our praying and at our Christian living by the help of His grace, and that we consciously direct all our powers to Him, until such time as, in all fullness of joy, we have Him whom we seek, Jesus.

Julian of Norwich[4]

Let nothing hinder us, nothing separate us, nothing disturb us. Let us all, everywhere and always, daily and constantly believe in [God] sincerely and humbly.

Francis of Assisi[5]

You must remain
    kneeling. Even as this moon
making its way through the earth's
cumbersome shadow, prayer, too,
has its phases.

R. S. Thomas[6]

INHERITING OUR PRESENT TIME

Grace doesn't travel along the paths known to us. Grace takes the road it fancies and it never takes the same road twice. Grace is free. It is the source of all freedom. When grace fails to rise like a spring of water, it may well be percolating surreptitiously.

Charles Péguy[1]

What happens when we pray is God's business, not ours. God will give us what He knows best. And what is best we see in the life of Jesus, in His joy and peace and stillness and confidence and trust. And also in His passion, His bloody sweat, His death and resurrection.

Harry Williams[2]

We know . . . that our poor attempt to pray is never wasted. We shall always come out of prayer different from when we started, but how and in what way we are different only God can tell.

Wendy Beckett[3]

Few people are actually able to inherit their present time because they are too stressed and rushed . . . Stillness is vital to the world of the soul. If, as you age, you become more still, you will discover that silence can be a great companion. The fragments of your life will have time to unify, the places where your soul shelter is wounded or broken will have time to knit and heal. You will be able to return to your self. In this stillness, you will engage your soul. Many people miss out on themselves completely as they journey through life. They know others, they know places, they know skills, they know their work, but tragically, they do not know themselves at all. Ageing can be a lovely time of ripening where you actually meet yourself, indeed maybe for the first time.

John O'Donohue[4]

The Spirit broods over the waters of our chaos, and out of chaos He brings order.

Mary Clare[5]

The spirit recreates . . . in a new pattern those among whom He is seen to dwell.

Cyril of Alexandria[6]

Companionship

My beloved is mine and I am his.
Song of Songs 2.16a

Companionship speaks of a maturity in love, a quiet intimacy, a friendship whose roots are buried deep in the soil of shared experiences. It is a familiar, congenial phase as people grow old in love and – in the best sense of the word – take each other for granted. Indeed, it is those who, having been lovers, can no longer be friends whose relationship becomes threadbare. And in the life of prayer nothing can express more simply the *companionship* which is one aspect of the language of love than the picture of the old peasant in the life of the Curé d'Ars who spent hours sitting in the chapel before the Blessed Sacrament and who, when questioned about what he was doing, merely replied, 'I look at Him, He looks at me, and we are happy.'[1]

But the *companionship* of prayer – in both the empathy and the activity of prayer – can never be confined to a personal piety. 'Souls – all human souls – are deeply interconnected.'[2] We might construct our lives in such a way that we deny the solidarity which nonetheless exists, the depth of belonging to which we are called; but prayer – properly understood, properly practised – brings out into the open, articulates the interdependence of our humanity. 'We are all most deeply interconnected . . . What happens to us when we pray is happening for men and women everywhere.'[3]

Any exposition of the *companionship* of prayer is bound to bring us therefore to some assessment of what we mean by intercession. It can be the most irksome of activities if it is confined to a repetition of names, of situations; but intercession – rightly understood – goes far beyond that. It is 'to *meet*, to *encounter*, to *be with someone* on behalf of or in relation to others'.[4] It is at one and the same time the most invigorating and – potentially – the most searching of prayers. 'Intercession means . . . to take a step that brings you to the centre of the conflict.'[5]

Intercession cannot easily take place unless patterns of waiting upon God have been established. 'To intercede is to bear others on the heart in God's presence.'[6] It is here that what has been called the empathy of prayer comes into its own. It is entering into the silence with another person in the mind and in the heart, so that – just for a moment – we stand where they stand, rejoicing or weeping with them. 'It is simply a matter of "being there for them" in a concentration upon the other which obliterates all awareness of self and yet it's not strung up but totally relaxed.'[7]

This suggests a degree of *companionship*, a depth of praying, which will not often be achieved by most of us; but what can be understood is the sense that 'living and praying are indivisible'.[8] One of the more sobering verses in the New Testament reminds us that 'anyone who does not love his brother whom he has seen, cannot love God whom he has not seen'.[9] If we are able to see the world – and those around us – through God's eyes, then it is a short step to grasping the truth. 'You can learn to love your brother or sister, if you only pray for them: and the longer you pray, the more you will love. I defy you to dislike anyone for whom you have prayed earnestly for any length of time.'[10]

But how far-reaching is this 'friendship for the friends of God'[11] which prayer can establish and sustain? Is our understanding of God and of His purposes confined to our humanity? Or is there a broader vision to which our generation is slowly becoming sensitive? If the *companionship* of prayer is an inescapable part of the language of love, is there now a compulsion about the passionate words of Father Zossima in his Discourses: 'Love men and women . . . Love all God's creation . . . Love every leaf . . . Love the animals . . . Love the plants . . . Love everything'?[12] And is the prize as rich as the word suggests: 'If you love everything you will perceive the divine mystery in things. Once you perceive it, you will begin to comprehend it better every day. And you will come to love the whole world with an all-embracing love'?[13]

DEEPLY INTERCONNECTED

We all know that we cannot separate ourselves at any time from the world to which we belong. There is no ultimate privacy or final isolation. We are always held and comprehended by something that is greater than we are, that has a claim upon us, and that demands a response from us.

Paul Tillich[1]

I wonder whether you realise a deep, great fact? That souls – all human souls – are deeply interconnected. That we cannot only pray for each other, but suffer for each other.

Baron von Hugel[2]

In the invisible world we are all most deeply interconnected ... What happens to us when we pray is happening for all men and women everywhere.

Harry Williams[3]

The whole of the past is involved in every human situation ... We never know whose love, whose prayers, whose fidelity in similar stress to some idea of good, brought up the strength to us to the amount available.

J. Neville Ward[4]

We don't really find out who we are until we find ourselves in Christ and in relation to other people.

Thomas Merton[5]

Everybody is my neighbour and my neighbour is myself.

Harry Williams[6]

CONTEMPLATIVE LIVING

In the life of the Curé d'Ars there is a story of an old peasant who used to spend hours and hours sitting in the Chapel motionless, doing nothing. The priest said to him, 'What are you doing all these hours?' The old peasant said, 'I look at Him, He looks at me, and we are happy'.

Curé d'Ars[1]

Words play very little part in this prayer . . .. Its main feature is that it is loving and looking, not discursive thinking.

J. Neville Ward[2]

God is friendship.

Aelred of Rievaulx[3]

We can only see His Face in others if we have gazed long at His Face in prayer.

Wendy Beckett[4]

The more we are alone with God the more we are united with one another.

Thomas Merton[5]

Only eyes that have sought Him in prayer see His presence in the day.

Wendy Beckett[6]

Contemplative living is really a matter of learning to see.

Alan Ecclestone[7]

Action is charity looking outward to other people, and contemplation is charity drawn inward to its own divine source.

Thomas Merton[8]

INTERCESSORY PRAYER

To intercede means literally not to make petitions or indeed to utter words at all but to *meet*, to *encounter*, to *be with someone* on behalf of or in relation to others.

Michael Ramsey[1]

Intercession means . . . to take a step that brings you to the centre of the conflict.

Anthony Bloom[2]

He who prays stands at that point of intersection where the love of God and the tensions and sufferings we inflict on each other meet and are held in the healing power of God.

Mary Clare[3]

The intercession of the Church is the offering of its will to participate, to uphold, to support.

W. H. Vanstone[4]

The intercession of the Church expresses our understanding of how costly a thing we are asking when we say, 'Thy will be done'.

W. H. Vanstone[5]

Intercession is an act to unite with God those who are unable to be united by themselves.

Thomas Merton[6]

THE EMPATHY OF PRAYER

Jesus on the Cross offered himself to humankind. Intercession is sharing in that offering of Jesus on the Cross for men and women.

Harry Williams[1]

To intercede is to bear others on the heart in God's presence.

Michael Ramsey[2]

Our intercession inevitably rebounds on us. It rebounds in two chief ways which are mysteriously intertwined – in pain and in joy. When we present somebody's need or pain to God we must be prepared in some way or other, in some degree or other, to share the pain.

Harry Williams[3]

We are not asked to bear the burden of humanity alone. We are only asked to realise that we cannot bear it alone. God bears it . . . Our only task is to ask for His help.

Wendy Beckett[4]

We are assisted in prayer by imaginative sympathy with the person for whom we pray or the situation about which we pray: we are assisted yet more by an understanding of that divine activity which is expended upon that person or that situation, of the extremity and costliness of its endeavour.

W. H. Vanstone[5]

To the full extent of my power, because I am a priest, I wish from now on to be the first to become conscious of all that the world loves, pursues and suffers; I want to be the first to seek, to sympathise and to suffer; the first to open myself out and sacrifice myself – to become more widely human and more nobly of the earth.

Teilhard de Chardin[6]

When someone whose life is simply and sacrificially dedicated to God has any fellow man or woman 'pretty constantly in mind' to the extent that the feeling of concern leads to responsible action, that, surely is the whole of intercession. For a timeless moment it makes one totally present with the other person or persons across the intervening distances, without words and in a manner that goes beyond thought. It is simply a matter of 'being there for them' in a concentration upon the other which obliterates all awareness of self and yet is not strung up but totally relaxed. In that stillness which lies beyond thought we are to let the presence of the other person impinge upon our spirit across the distance, with all his or her rich reality and all his or her need and burden. His or her presence matters more than our own.

John V. Taylor[7]

LIVING AND PRAYING

If God is life, then the person who does not see Him does not see life.

Gregory of Nyssa[1]

Prayer and life, living and praying, are indivisible.

Mary Clare[2]

Prayer is the search for a relationship.

Mary Clare[3]

For nothing among human things has such power to keep our gaze fixed ever more intensely upon God, than friendship for the friends of God.

Simone Weil[4]

You can learn to love your brother or sister, if you only pray for them: and the longer you pray, the more you will love. I defy you to dislike anyone for whom you have prayed earnestly for any length of time.

Forbes Robinson[5]

We can bear all things provided we possess Christ Jesus dwelling within us as our friend and affectionate guide.

Teresa of Avila[6]

Christian prayer involves in various ways our making repeated approaches to the meaning of life as Jesus lived it.

J. Neville Ward[7]

EYES OPEN TO THE WORLD

Holiness means seeing the world through His eyes.

Wendy Beckett[1]

Prayer must be fashioning a Yes to God that works out in the life of the whole world what such a faith entails.

Alan Ecclestone[2]

O Lord, remember not only the men and women of good will but also those of ill will.

Do not remember all the suffering they have inflicted on us: remember the fruit we bear thanks to this suffering – our comradeship; our loyalty; our humility, courage, generosity, the greatness of heart which has grown out of all this.

And when they come to judgement let all the fruit we have borne be their forgiveness.

Anonymous[3]

The only power that we have, the only power that is real, the only power that endures, the only power that transforms and transcends is the power to love, and that power is made perfect in what and whom we forgive.

Peter Gomes[4]

Hands open to God, eyes open to the world; and within, the hidden energy that soaks the Church with divine action, divine love.

Rowan Williams[5]

AN ALL-EMBRACING LOVE

We should try to bear in our hearts the whole world . . .
This is the highest charity. They love me best who love
me in their prayers.

J. C. Ryle[1]

He prayeth well, who loveth well
Both man and bird and beast.

He prayeth best, who loveth best
All things both great and small.

Samuel Taylor Coleridge[2]

The eye that sees nobility and beauty in what another would
regard as ordinary is the eye of prayer. Only in the light
of Jesus can we see the fullness of creation.

Wendy Beckett[3]

Brothers, have no fear of people's sin. Love men and women
even in their sin, for that is the semblance of divine love
and is the highest love on earth. Love all God's creation, the
whole and every grain of sand in it. Love every leaf and every
ray of God's light. Love the animals, love the plants, love
everything. If you love everything you will perceive the divine
mystery in things. Once you perceive it, you will begin to comprehend it better every day. And you will come at last to love
the whole world with an all-embracing love.

Fyodor Dostoyevsky[4]

Abandonment

Set me as a seal upon your heart, as a seal upon your arm;
for love is strong as death.
Song of Songs 8.6

Awareness, exploration, passion, pain, patience, companionship – and *abandonment*. There are countless 'deaths' along the way in any relationship where growth is taking place. Passion, pain and patience all have their stories to tell. But there is a final *abandonment*, an irreversible letting go, in the relationships of those who love as old age, infirmity and death overtake us.

Abandonment is nonetheless a word that properly belongs to prayer as the language of love. The pattern to be discovered, explored, replicated is the pattern of Christ Himself. What it means for us in our discipleship to be handed over, to let go, to give ourselves away, will vary a good deal from person to person. The poverty of our discipleships may be so far removed from any such ideal that it becomes ludicrous to talk in such terms. But if the pattern to which we aspire – even as we fall short – is nothing less than that of Christ, then it must follow that 'the deepest prayer at its nub is a perpetual surrender to God'.[1]

It is impossible to talk about *abandonment* without bringing into play all the resonances associated with the story of Holy Week and Easter Day. If 'the reality central to my life is the life of God';[2] if 'the way to God lies through deep darkness';[3] if 'He who died for me is all that I seek';[4] then that central mystery of death and resurrection, which is the gospel, will be played out again and again as life unfolds.

The resonances – the echoes – of Christ's passion, death and resurrection speak of self-giving but of doing so in freedom, in confidence and in trust. 'My true identity lies hidden in God's call to my freedom and my response to Him.'[5] Here again the parallels can be drawn between the relationships of love and the activity of prayer. The call to love – like the call to prayer – is always an invitation to enter into life; but life – if it is lived to the full – necessarily involves an *abandonment* at different points along the way. 'The Yes to God of prayer not only gathers up all things that are . . . but launches out the one who prays into the deeps . . . It involves us no less in going on further to the yet unspoken, unseen, unimaginable Yes whither He has gone before."[6]

GOD'S CALL TO MY FREEDOM

Always remember that whether you are alive or dead it matters nothing. What matters is what you live for and what you are prepared to die for.

Anthony Bloom[1]

Yet am I sure that the meaning of my life is the meaning God intends for it? Does God impose a meaning on my life from the *outside*, through event, custom, routine, law, system, impact with others in society? Or am I called to *create from within*, with Him, with His Grace, a meaning which reflects His truth and makes me His 'word' spoken freely in my personal situation?

Thomas Merton[2]

True perfection, the only perfection, does not mean leading this or that kind of life, but doing the will of God; it means leading the kind of life that God wills, and where He wills, and leading it as He would have led it Himself.

Charles de Foucauld[3]

The reality central to my life is the life of God.

Thomas Merton[4]

My true identity lies hidden in God's call to my freedom and my response to him.

Thomas Merton[5]

A PERPETUAL SURRENDER

The deepest prayer at its nub is a perpetual surrender to
God.

Thomas Merton[1]

If prayer is learning to unite our wills with the will of God,
then the cost must be the cost of calvary.

Mary Clare[2]

The cross means sharing the suffering of Christ to the last
and to the fullest.

Dietrich Bonhoeffer[3]

Unless we are ready and willing to die in conformity with
His passion, His life is not in us.

Ignatius of Antioch[4]

He died from what was ours, we will live from what is
His.

Augustine of Hippo[5]

Prayer and sacrifice support and require each other.

Thomas Merton[6]

Suffer with Christ and for Christ, if you desire to reign with
Christ.

Thomas à Kempis[7]

DYING OF A LOVE THAT LOOKS LIKE DEATH

The universe is the totality of being for which God gives Himself in love.

W. H. Vanstone[1]

It is in solitude, in this living with God, alone with God, in this profound withdrawal of the soul within itself, forgetful of all created things, that God gives Himself wholly to whomever gives himself wholly to Him.

Charles de Foucauld[2]

Have we ever tried to love God where no wave of emotional enthusiasm bears us up and we can no longer confuse ourselves and our life-urge with God, where we seem to be dying of a love that looks like death and absolute negation and we appear to be calling out into nothingness and the utterly unrequited?

Karl Rahner[3]

When we pray, we are being united with Jesus Christ in his own redemptive action; we are being drawn into the great cosmic battle against evil, which is to bring into the here and now of our daily lives the fruits of Christ's victorious passion.

Mary Clare[4]

To conform to the will of God is to contribute to the healing of the world; to depart from it is to add to the chain of evil which weighs upon us all.

Paul Tournier[5]

The conclusion is always the same: love is the most powerful and still the most unknown energy of the world.

Pierre Teilhard de Chardin[6]

THE YES TO GOD

... a wordless and total surrender of the heart in silence.

Thomas Merton[1]

The Yes to God of prayer not only gathers up all things that are, the light and dark, the pain and joy, the ventures and the failures, life and death, but launches out the one who prays into the deeps transcending these. In prayer we answer yes to what we've managed to face in life so far by learning to share in the Yes in Christ. It involves us no less in going on further to the yet unspoken, unseen, unimaginable Yes whither He has gone before.

Alan Ecclestone[2]

He kneeled down
   dismissing his orisons
as inappropriate ; one by one
  they came to his lips and were swallowed
but without bile.
  He fell back
on an old prayer: Teach me to know
  what to pray for. He
listened ; after the weather of
  his asking, no still, small
voice, only the parade
  of ghosts, casualties
of his past intercessions. He
  held out his hands, cupped
as though to receive blood, leaking
  from life's side. They

remained dry, as his mouth
   did. But the prayer formed:
Deliver me from the long drought
   of the mind. Let leaves
from the deciduous Cross
   fall on us, washing
us clean, turning our autumn
   to gold by the affluence of their fountain.

R. S. Thomas[3]

I give you the end of a golden string:
   Only wind it into a ball,
It will lead you in at Heaven's Gate,
   Built in Jerusalem's Wall.

William Blake[4]

LIVING AND DYING WITH THE BELOVED

Of all that God has done in and for the world the most glorious thing is this – that He has handed Himself over to the world.

W. H. Vanstone[1]

The time is now, the place is here, the time of life is today.

Dorothy Soelle[2]

Now the greatest power of love is this, that even when spurned the One who loves is willing to live and die with the beloved.

John Chrysostom[3]

It is written of me
That I should do your will,
O my God.

This is my Father's will,
That I lay down my life
And take it again.

Such is the work of love
Between Father and Son
In one Spirit.

Anonymous[4]

Christ pierced on the Cross is 'the very book of love' laid open before us.

Lancelot Andrewes[5]

Where the lamb died
 a bird sings.
Where a soul perishes
what music? The Cross

is an old-fashioned
weapon, but its bow
is drawn unerringly
against the heart.

R. S. Thomas[6]

THROUGH DEEP DARKNESS

The way to God lies through deep darkness.

Thomas Merton[1]

Dark, dark, dark.
  is the waiting heart
but in the darkness
  Light
Light of Christ
  Christ
Light of the world.

Anonymous[2]

To one kneeling down no word came.
  Only the wind's song, saddening the lips
Of the grave saints, rigid in glass ;
Or the dry whisper of unseen wings,
Bats not angels, in the high roof.

Was he balked by silence? He kneeled long,
And saw love in a dark crown
Of thorns blazing, and a winter tree
Golden with fruit of a man's body.

R. S. Thomas[3]

What I promise, I give; what I have said, I will perform,
  provided you remain faithful in My love to the end.

Thomas à Kempis[4]

Not the empty tomb
but the uninhabited
cross. Look long enough
and you will see the arms
put on leaves. Not a crown
of thorns, but a crown of flowers
haloing it, with a bird singing
as though perched on paradise's threshold.

R. S. *Thomas*[5]

MY WHOLE DESIRE

You would know our Lord's meaning? Know it well. Love was His meaning. Who showed it you? Love. What did He show you? Love. Why did He show it? For love. Hold on to this and you will know and understand love more and more. But you will not know or learn anything else – ever!

Julian of Norwich[1]

He who died for us is all that I seek; He who rose again for us is my whole desire.

Ignatius of Antioch[2]

Upon Christ throw all away:
know ye, this is Easter Day.

Pluck the harp and breathe the horn:
know ye not 'tis Easter morn.

Earth throws Winter's robes away,
Decks herself for Easter Day.

Open wide your hearts that they
let in joy this Easter Day.

Henceforth let your souls alway
Make each morn an Easter Day.

Gerard Manley Hopkins[3]

Come, my Way, my Truth, my Life:
Such a Way, as gives us breath;
Such a Truth, as ends all strife;
And such a Life, as killeth death.

Come, my Light, my Feast, my Strength:
Such a Light, as shows a feast;
Such a Feast, as mends in length;
Such a Strength, as makes his guest.

Come, my Joy, my Love, my Heart:
Such a Joy, as none can move;
Such a Love, as none can part;
Such a Heart, as joyes in love.

George Herbert[4]

Notes and References

Preface

1   J. Neville Ward, *The Use of Praying*, Epworth Press, 1962, p. 12.
2   *The Prose Works of Thomas Ken*, 1838, pp. 380–1.
3   R. S. Thomas, *Counterpoint*, Bloodaxe Books, 1993, p. 63.
4   Alan Ecclestone, *Yes to God*, Darton, Longman & Todd, 1976, p. 8.
5   Matthew 13.52.
6   Alan Ecclestone, *Yes to God*, p. 21.
7   Mother Mary Clare, *Encountering the Depths,* Darton, Longman & Todd, 1981, p. 4.
8   George Herbert, 'Prayer (1)'.
9   Sister Wendy Beckett, *The Gaze of Love,* Marshall Pickering, 1993, p. 28.
10 Dorothee Soelle, *The Silent Cry*, trans. Martin Rumscheidt, Fortress Press, 2001, p. 296.
11 Basil Hume, *Searching for God*, Hodder & Stoughton, 1979, p. 31.
12 Mother Mary Clare, *Encountering the Depths,* p. 4.
13 Dorothee Soelle, *The Silent Cry*, p. 296.
14 J. Neville Ward, *The Use of Praying*, p. 54.
15 Matthew 6.6.
16 John 17.24.
17 John 3.16.
18 John 13.1.
19 1 John 3.16.
20 1 John 3.14.
21 Romans 8.38–9.
22 1 Corinthians 13.7.
23 Source unknown.
24 J. Neville Ward, *Friday Afternoon*, Epworth Press, 1982, p. 82.
25 Thomas à Kempis, *The Imitation of Christ*, Book 3, Chapter 5.

Awareness

1 R. S. Thomas, 'The Porch', Collected Poems 1945–1990, J. M. Dent, 1993, p. 326.
2 Mother Mary Clare, *Encountering the Depths*, p. 4.
3 William Blake, *Auguries of Innocence*.
4 Thomas Merton, *Conjecture of a Guilty Bystander*, Image Books, 1968, p. 308.
5 St Augustine of Hippo, *Homilies on St John's Gospel*, Hom. 26, 4–6.
6 John O'Donohue, *Anam Cara: Spiritual Wisdom from the Celtic World*, Bantam Press, 1998, p. 28.

God's Activity in Us

1 Mother Mary Clare, *Encountering the Depths,* p. 4.
2 Bayezid Bistani, Sofi mystic of the ninth century, cited by Dorothee Soelle, *The Silent Cry*, p. 17.
3 Source unknown.
4 H. A. Williams, *The Joy of God*, Mitchell Beazley, 1979, p. 31.
5 Thomas Merton, *The Monastic Journey*, ed. Patrick Hart, Image Books, 1978, p. 223.
6 John O'Donohue, *Anam Cara*, p. 28.

The Inward Journey

1 Michael Mayne, *A Year Lost and Found*, Darton, Longman & Todd, 1987, p. 70.
2 R. S. Thomas, 'Groping', *Collected Poems*.
3 Alan Ecclestone, *Yes to God*, p. 30.
4 Renée Voillaume, *The Living God*, Darton, Longman & Todd, 1980, p. 86.
5 Sister Wendy Beckett, *The Gaze of Love,* p. 92.
6 Basil Hume, *Searching for God*, p. 31.

Drawn by Delight

1 John O'Donohue, *Anam Cara*, p. 17.

2 T. S. Eliot, 'East Coker', *Collected Poems 1909–1962*, Faber & Faber, 1963.

3 Meister Eckhart, *Sermons*. Cited by Oliver Davies, *Meister Eckhart: Mystical Theologian*, SPCK, 1991, p. 170.

4 John O'Donohue, *Anam Cara*, p. 104.

5 St Augustine of Hippo, *Homilies on St John's Gospel*, Hom. 26, 4–6.

6 John Hare, Bishop of Bedford 1968–76. From a sermon preached at Clapham church, 20 September 1976.

7 R. S. Thomas, 'AD', *Counterpoint*.

One Life in God

1 Simone Weil, *Waiting on God*, Collins: Fontana Books, 1959, p. 40.

2 Jan van Ruysbroeck, *The Twelve Beguines*, iv, 30.

3 William Blake, *Auguries of Innocence*.

4 Dorothee Soelle, *The Silent Cry*, p. 185.

5 Friedrich Nietzsche. Cited by Paul Tillich, *The Shaking of the Foundations*, SCM Press, 1957, p. 63.

Stretching Hearts Wide Open

1 Isaac of Stella, *Sermons*, Sermon 31.

2 St John Chrysostom, *Homilies*, Hom. 13, 1–2.

3 John A. T. Robinson, *Honest to God*, SCM Press, 1963, p. 100.

4 Antiphon at the Washing of the Feet on Maundy Thursday.

The Language Of Love

1 Dorothee Soelle, *The Silent Cry*, p. 296.

2 Father Richard Benson.

3 St Augustine of Hippo, *Sermons*, Sermon 34, 1–3, 5–6.

4 St Augustine of Hippo, *Homilies on St John's Gospel*, Tr. 34, 8–9.

5 John O'Donohue, *Anam Cara*, pp. 27–8.

6 John O'Donohue, *Anam Cara*, p. 26.

7 Alan Ecclestone, *Yes to God*, p. 38.
8 Basil Hume, *Searching for God*, p. 31.

Start Where You Are

1 Alan Ecclestone, *Yes to God*, p. 21.
2 Austin Farrer, *The End of Man*, SPCK, 1973.
3 Boris Pasternak. Cited by John O'Donohue, *Anam Cara*, p. 29.
4 Maria Boulding.
5 Mother Mary Clare, *Encountering the Depths,* p. 5.
6 Julian of Norwich, *Revelations of Divine Love.*
7 Sister Wendy Beckett, *The Gaze of Love*, p. 26.
8 Thomas Merton, *Thomas Merton: A Monastic Tribute*, ed. Patrick Hart, Hodder & Stoughton, 1974, p. 80.

Exploration

1 Alan Ecclestone, *Yes to God*, p. 94.
2 St Augustine of Hippo.
3 Alan Ecclestone, *Yes to God*, p. 123.
4 Sister Wendy Beckett, *The Gaze of Love,* p. 10.
5 Mother Mary Clare, *Encountering the Depths,* p. 13.
6 R. S. Thomas, 'Incarnation', *Counterpoint.*
7 Father Herbert Kelly, *Principles*, SSM Press, 1957, Section IX.
8 Catherine de Hueck Doherty.
9 Thomas Merton, *The New Man*, Harcourt Brace Jovanovich, 1995, p. 25.
10 Cyprian, *On the Lord's Prayer*, N. 8–9.

Unreality and Dreams

1 Austin Farrer, *The End of Man.*
2 Thomas Merton, *Contemplative Prayer*, Darton, Longman & Todd, 1975, p. 9.
3 Simone Weil, *Waiting on God*, p. 115.
4 Thomas Merton, *A Monastic Tribute*, p. 81.
5 Alan Ecclestone, *On Praying*, Prism Publications; reprinted in *Spirituality for Today*, ed. Eric James, SCM Press, 1968.

Finding Our Way

1 Anthony Bloom, *School for Prayer*, Darton, Longman & Todd, 1970, p. 2.
2 Thomas Merton, *No Man Is an Island*, Harcourt Brace Jovanovich, 1955, p. 25.
3 Father Andrew.
4 Alan Ecclestone, *Yes to God*, p. 7.
5 Alan Ecclestone, *Yes to God*, p. 94.
6 Alan Ecclestone, *Yes to God*, pp. 123–4.
7 Dorothee Soelle, *The Silent Cry*, p. 294.

Our Deepest Freedom

1 Thomas Merton, *Contemplation in a World of Action*, Image Books 1973, p. 344.
2 Thomas Merton, *The Hidden Ground of Love: The Letters of Thomas Merton on Religious Experience and Social Concern*, ed. William H Shannon, Farrar, Strauss, Giroux, 1985, p. 159.
3 Dorothee Soelle, *The Silent Cry*, p. 296.
4 Sister Wendy Beckett, *The Gaze of Love*, p. 10.
5 Alan Ecclestone, *Yes to God*, p. 8.
6 Charles de Foucauld. Cited by Brother Kenneth CGA. *From the Fathers to the Churches*, Collins, 1985, p. 165.
7 Karl Barth, *Church Dogmatics*, T & T Clark, 1975, Vol I, Part I p. 465.

The Simplest Way

1 Sister Wendy Beckett, *The Gaze of Love*, p. 9.
2 Thomas Merton, *A Monastic Tribute*, p. 79.
3 Alan Ecclestone, *Yes to God*, p. 19.
4 Meister Eckhart, *Sermons*. Cited by Oliver Davies, *Meister Eckhart*, p. 168.
5 Tertullian, *On Prayer*, Chapters 28–9.
6 St John of the Cross. Cited by Dorothee Soelle, *The Silent Cry*, p. 217.

Superfluous Words

1 St Augustine of Hippo, *From the Letter to Proba*, Ep. 130.20.
2 St Augustine of Hippo, *From the Letter to Proba*, Ep. 130. 11.
3 Alessandro Pronzato, *Meditations on the Sand*, St Paul Publications, 1982, p. 92.

The Silent Language of Love

1 Father Herbert Kelly, *Principles*, Section IX.
2 Mother Teresa of Calcutta.
3 Jean Sullivan.
4 St John of the Cross, *Complete Works*, ed. E. Allison Peers, Burns Oates and Washbourne, 1935, Vol. III, p. 255.
5 Catherine de Hueck Doherty.
6 John O'Donohue, *Anam Cara*, p. 99.

One in God

1 Thomas Merton, *New Seeds of Contemplation*, New Directions, 1962, p. 267.
2 H. A. Williams, *The Joy of God*, p. 27.
3 Thomas Merton. Cited by Brother Kenneth, *From the Fathers to the Churches*, p. 612.
4 St Cyprian, *On the Lord's Prayer*, N. 8–9.
5 Thomas Merton, *A Monastic Tribute*, p. 88.
6 George Herbert, 'Prayer (1)'.
7 Alan Ecclestone, *Yes to God*, p. 125.

Passion

1 Samuel Chadwick, *The Gospel of the Cross*, London, 1934, p. 17.
2 Thomas Merton, *The Monastic Journey*, p. 21.
3 Thomas à Kempis, *The Imitation of Christ*, Book 3, Chapter 5.
4 Thomas à Kempis, *The Imitation of Christ*, Book 3, Chapter 5.
5 1 Corinthians 13.7.
6 Sister Wendy Beckett, *The Gaze of Love*, p. 44.

7 George MacDonald, *Wilfred Cumbermede*, 1872.
8 Anthony Bloom, *School for Prayer*, p. 30.
9 Alan Ecclestone, *Yes to God*, p. 10.
10 Thomas Ken, *An Exposition of the Church Catechism*.

A Living Flame

1 Thomas à Kempis, *The Imitation of Christ*, Book 3, Chapter 5.
2 Meister Eckhart, *Sermons*. Cited by Oliver Davies, *Meister Eckhart*, p. 151.
3 Michel Quoist, *Prayers of Life*, Gill & Son, 1966, p. 112.
4 Michel Quoist, *Prayers of Life*, p. 32.
5 Thomas Merton, *The Monastic Garden*, ed. Patrick Hart, Image Books, 1978, p. 21.

A Fire Ever Burning

1 St Catherine of Siena, *Dialogue*, Chapter 167.
2 Meister Eckhart. Cited by Dorothee Soelle, *The Silent Cry*, p. 21.
3 St Augustine of Hippo, *Confessions*, Book 10, 26, 37.

Total Love: Total Truth

1 Thomas Ken, *An Exposition of the Church Catechism*.
2 Simone Weil. Cited by Dorothee Soelle, *The Silent Cry*, p. 151.
3 Dorothee Soelle, *The Silent Cry*, p. 6.
4 Sister Wendy Beckett, *The Gaze of Love*, p. 9.
5 Sister Wendy Beckett, *The Gaze of Love*, p. 50.
6 Anthony Bloom, *School for Prayer*, p. xv.
7 Sister Wendy Beckett, *The Gaze of Love*, p. 44.

Singing the Song of Love

1 Thomas à Kempis, *The Imitation of Christ*, Book 3, Chapter 5.
2 Sister Wendy Beckett, *The Gaze of Love*, p. 28.
3 Sister Wendy Beckett, *The Gaze of Love*, p. 44.
4 John O'Donohue, *Anam Cara*, p. 246.

5 Christopher Fry, *One Thing More: Caedmon Construed*, printed privately, 1986, pp. 53–4.

6 Thomas à Kempis, *The Imitation of Christ*, Book 3, Chapter 5.

Plumbing New Depths

1 Thomas Traherne, *Centuries of Meditation*. Cited by Brother Kenneth, *From the Fathers to the Churches*, pp. 434–5.

2 Alan Ecclestone, *Yes to God*, p. 31.

3 John O'Donohue, *Anam Cara*, p. 60.

4 Sister Wendy Beckett, *The Gaze of Love*, pp. 10–11.

5 W. H. Vanstone, *Love's Endeavour, Love's Expense*, Darton, Longman & Todd, 1979, p. 45.

6 W. H. Vanstone, *Love's Endeavour, Love's Expense*, p. 50.

7 John O'Donohue, *Anam Cara*, p. 15.

The Door of the Kingdom

1 St John Chrysostom. Cited by Anthony Bloom, *School for Prayer*, p. 19.

2 W. H. Vanstone, *The Stature of Waiting*, Darton, Longman & Todd, 1984, p. 96.

3 Thomas à Kempis, *The Imitation of Christ*, Book 1, Chapter 15.

4 Anthony Bloom, *School for Prayer*, p. 30.

5 Alan Ecclestone, *Yes to God*, p. 10.

Love's Energy Working Love

1 John O'Donohue, *Anam Cara*, p. 37.

2 W. H. Vanstone, *The Stature of Waiting*, pp. 95–6.

3 St Augustine of Hippo, *Sermons*, Sermon 23A, 1.

4 Sister Wendy Beckett, *The Gaze of Love*, p. 48.

5 St Benedict.

6 R. S. Thomas, Theophanies.

7 Office Hymn at Terce, St Mary's Abbey, West Malling.

Pain

1   Mother Mary Clare, *Encountering the Depths,* p. 5.
2   Rowan Williams, *Ponder These Things,* Canterbury Press, 2002, p. 49.
3   Luke 18.14.
4   R. S. Thomas, 'Via Negativa', *Collected Poems.*
5   Anthony Bloom, *School for Prayer,* p. xvii.
6   St Nicholas of Flue.
7   J. Neville Ward, *The Use of Praying,* pp. 144–5.
8   J. Neville Ward, *The Use of Praying,* p. 88.
9   Thomas Merton, *The Climate of Monastic Prayer.* Cited by Mother Mary Clare, *Encountering the Depths,* p. 44.
10 Mother Mary Clare, *Encountering the Depths,* p. 12.

That Great Absence

1   R. S. Thomas, 'Via Negativa', *Collected Poems.*
2   Anthony Bloom, *School for Prayer,* p. xvii.

Even When it is Night

1   R. S. Thomas, 'Migrants', *Mass for Hard Times,* Bloodaxe Books, 1992, p. 80.
2   St John of the Cross. Cited by Dorothee Soelle, *The Silent Cry,* p. 143.

Living a Dying Life

1   St Nicholas of Flue.
2   Basil Hume, *Searching for God,* p. 107.
3   Thomas Merton, *Contemplative Prayer,* p. 8.
4   Mother Mary Clare, *Encountering the Depths,* p. 12.
5   Thomas à Kempis, *The Imitation of Christ,* Book 2, Chapter 12.

The Essential Heart of Prayer

1 J. Neville Ward, *The Use of Praying*, pp. 144–5.
2 Mother Mary Clare, *Encountering the Depths*, p. 5.
3 Alan Ecclestone, *Yes to God*, p. 105.

Deep into The Heart of the World

1 Thomas Merton, *The Climate of Monastic Prayer*. Cited by Mother Mary Clare, *Encountering the Depths*, p. 44.
2 J. Neville Ward, *The Use of Praying*, p. 89.
3 Thomas Merton, *Contemplative Prayer*, p. 25.
4 Dietrich Bonhoeffer, *Letters and Papers from Prison*, SCM Press, 1967, p. 186.
5 Dorothee Soelle, *The Silent Cry*, p. 87.
6 St John of the Cross. Cited by Dorothee Soelle, *The Silent Cry*, p. 140.

Watching With Christ

1 Sister Wendy Beckett, *The Gaze of Love*, p. 66.
2 Evelyn Underhill, *Life as Prayer (Collected Papers)*, Morehouse, repr. 1991, pp. 57–9.
3 Don Helder Camara.
4 Dietrich Bonhoeffer, *Letters and Papers from Prison*, p. 300.
5 J. Neville Ward, *The Use of Praying*, p. 88.
6 Dorothee Soelle, *The Silent Cry*, p. 138.

Sit Down and Taste My Meat

1 Michel Quoist, *Prayers of Life*, pp. 110–11.
2 George Herbert, 'Love (III)'.

Patience

1 W. H. Vanstone, *Love's Endeavour, Love's Expense*, p. 34.
2 R. S. Thomas, 'The Moon in Lleyn', *Collected Poems*.
3 St Clare.

4 Ladislaus Boros, *The Cosmic Christ*, trans. David Smith, Search Press, 1975, pp. 52–3.

5 Thomas Merton, *The Hidden Ground of Love: The Letters of Thomas Merton on Religious Experience and Social Concerns*, ed. William H. Shannon, Farrar, Straus, Giroux, 1985, p. 371.

6 Origen. Cited by Mother Mary Clare, *Encountering the Depths*, p. 20.

7 A Monk, *The Hermitage Within*, Darton, Longman & Todd, 1977, p. 7.

8 Mother Teresa of Calcutta. Cited by Mother Mary Clare, *Encountering the Depths*, p. 23.

9 Thomas Merton. Cited by Brother Kenneth, *From the Fathers to the Churches*, p. 612.

10 Rowan Williams, *Ponder These Things*, p. 53.

11 St Augustine of Hippo, Treatise on St John, Tr. 17, 7–9.

12 Colossians 3.3.

13 John O'Donohue, *Anam Cara*, p. 235.

14 R. S. Thomas, 'Tidal', *Mass for Hard Times*, p. 43.

15 Thomas Merton, *A Monastic Tribute*, p. 81.

16 Mother Mary Clare, *Encountering the Depths*, p. 17.

17 St Teresa of Avila. Found in St Teresa's breviary after her death. Cited by Elizabeth Hamilton, *The Servants of Love: The Spirituality of Teresa of Avila*, Darton, Longman & Todd, 1975, p. 103.

18 Sister Wendy Beckett, *The Gaze of Love*, p. 62.

The Inner Hermitage

1 A Monk, *The Hermitage Within*, p. 7.

2 Cited by F. C. Happold, *Religious Faith and Twentieth Century Man*, Darton, Longman and Todd, 1980, p. 170.

3 Mother Mary Clare, *Encountering the Depths*, p. 71.

4 John O'Donohue, *Anam Cara*, p. 154.

A Time of Waiting

1 Thomas Merton, *The Hidden Ground of Love*, p. 371.

2 St Clare.

3 Ladislaus Boros, *The Cosmic Christ*, pp. 52–3.

4 Paul Tillich, *The Shaking of the Foundations*, SCM Press, 1957, p. 152.
5 Paul Tillich, *The Shaking of the Foundations*, p. 152.
6 St Teresa of Avila. Found in St Teresa's breviary after her death. Cited by Elizabeth Hamilton, *The Servants of Love: The Spirituality of Teresa of Avila*, Darton, Longman & Todd, 1975, p. 103.

Looking and Listening

1 R. S. Thomas, 'Sea-Watching', *Collected Poems*.
2 Rowan Williams, *Ponder These Things*, p. 53.
3 St Augustine of Hippo, *Treatises on St John*, Tr. 17, 7–9.
4 Dietrich Bonhoeffer, *Life Together*, Harper SanFrancisco, 1978 (originally published 1938).

To Pray True

1 Mother Teresa of Calcutta. Cited by Mother Mary Clare, *Encountering the Depths*, p. 23.
2 R. S. Thomas, 'The Letter', *Mass for Hard Times*, p. 77.
3 Isaac of Nineveh. Cited by Thomas Merton, *Contemplative Prayer*, Darton, Longman & Todd, 1975, p. 33.
4 P. A. H. de Boer, *Fatherhood and Motherhood in Israelite and Judaean Piety*, F. S. Brill, 1947, p. 53.
5 St John of the Cross. Cited by Dorothee Soelle, *The Silent Cry*, p. 73.
6 Thomas Merton, *Contemplative Prayer*, Image Books, 1971, p. 90.
7 Origen. Cited by Mother Mary Clare, *Encountering the Depths*, p. 20.

The Courage to Face Myself

1 John O'Donohue, *Anam Cara*, p. 145.
2 Thomas Merton. Cited by Brother Kenneth, *From the Fathers to the Churches*, p. 612.
3 Thomas Merton, *Contemplative Prayer*, Darton, Longman & Todd, 1975, p. 44.

4 H. A. Williams, *Becoming What I Am*, Darton, Longman & Todd, 1977, p. 58.
5 William Temple, *Christian Faith and Life*, SCM Press, p. 36.
6 St John Chrysostom, *Homilies on Acts of the Apostles*, Hom. 20.4.
7 St Ignatius of Antioch, *Letter to the Romans*, 6, 1–9, 3.

Let Nothing Hinder Me

1 Mother Mary Clare, *Encountering the Depths*, p. 17.
2 R. S. Thomas, *Tidal*.
3 Thomas Merton, *A Monastic Tribute*, p. 81.
4 Mother Julian of Norwich, *Revelations of Divine Love*.
5 St Francis of Assisi, *A Reading from the First Rule of Francis of Assisi*.
6 R. S. Thomas, 'The Moon in Lleyn', *Collected Poems*.

Inheriting Our Present Time

1 Charles Péguy. Cited by H A Williams, *The Joy of God*, p. 127.
2 H. A. Williams, *Becoming What I Am*, p. 49.
3 Sister Wendy Beckett, *The Gaze of Love*, p. 62.
4 John O' Donohue, *Anam Cara*, pp. 234–5.
5 Mother Mary Clare, *Encountering the Depths*, p. 37.
6 St Cyril of Alexandria, *Commentary on St John's Gospel*, Book 10.

Companionship

1 Curé d'Ars. Cited by Anthony Bloom, *School for Prayer*, p. 62.
2 Baron von Hugel, *Letters to a Niece*, J. M. Dent & Sons, 1928. p. 25.
3 H. A. Williams, *Becoming What I Am*, p. 47.
4 Michael Ramsey.
5 Anthony Bloom, *God and Man*, Darton, Longman & Todd, 1971, p. 44.
6 Michael Ramsey.
7 John V. Taylor, *The Go-Between God*, SCM Press, 1972, p. 242.

8 Mother Mary Clare, *Encountering the Depths,* p. 13.
9 1 John 4.20b.
10 Forbes Robinson, *College and Ordination Addresses,* ed. Charles H. Robinson, Longman Grace & Co., 1905, p. 172.
11 Simone Weil, *Waiting on God,* p. 40.
12 Fyodor Dostoyevsky, *The Brothers Karamazov,* Penguin Books, 1985, p. 375.
13 Fyodor Dostoyevsky, *The Brothers Karamazov,* Penguin Books, 1985, p. 375.

Deeply Interconnected

1 Paul Tillich, *The Shaking of the Foundations,* p. 46.
2 Baron von Hugel, *Letters to a Niece,* p. 25.
3 H. A. Williams, *Becoming What I Am,* p. 47.
4 J. Neville Ward, *Friday Afternoon,* Epworth Press, 1982, p. 17.
5 Thomas Merton, *The New Man,* Mentor Omega, 1963, p. 46.
6 H. A. Williams, *Becoming What I Am,* p. 11.

Contemplative Living

1 Curé d'Ars. Cited by Anthony Bloom, *School for Prayer,* p. 62.
2 J. Neville Ward, *The Use of Praying,* p. 36.
3 St Aelred of Rievaulx, *De Spirituali Amicitia i.*
4 Sister Wendy Beckett, *The Gaze of Love,* p. 58.
5 Thomas Merton, *Seeds of Contemplation,* Dell, 1949, p. 33.
6 Sister Wendy Beckett, *The Gaze of Love,* p. 82.
7 Alan Ecclestone, *Yes to God,* p. 40.
8 Thomas Merton, *No Man Is an Island,* p. 70.

Intercessory Prayer

1 Michael Ramsey.
2 Anthony Bloom, *God and Man,* p. 44.
3 Mother Mary Clare.
4 W. H. Vanstone, *Love's Endeavour, Love's Expense,* p. 110.
5 W. H. Vanstone, *Love's Endeavour, Love's Expense,* p. 111.
6 Thomas Merton.

The Empathy of Prayer

1 H. A. Williams, *Becoming What I Am*, Darton, Longman & Todd, 1977, p. 73.
2 Michael Ramsey.
3 H. A. Williams, *Becoming What I Am*, p. 72.
4 Sister Wendy Beckett, *The Gaze of Love*, p. 106.
5 W. H. Vanstone, *Love's Endeavour, Love's Expense*, pp. 110–11.
6 Teilhard de Chardin, *Le Prêtre*. Cited by Eric James, *Odd Man Out?*, Hodder & Stoughton, 1962, p. 45.
7 John V. Taylor, *The Go-Between God*, p. 242.

Living and Praying

1 St Gregory of Nyssa, *Homilies on the Beatitudes*, Or. 6.
2 Mother Mary Clare, *Encountering the Depths*, p. 13.
3 Mother Mary Clare, *Encountering the Depths*, p. 5.
4 Simone Weil, *Waiting on God*, p. 40.
5 Forbes Robinson, *College and Ordination Addresses*, p. 172.
6 St Teresa of Avila, *The Book of Life*, Ch. 22.6.
7 J. Neville Ward, *Friday Afternoon*, p. 82.

Eyes Open to the World

1 Sister Wendy Beckett, *The Gaze of Love*, p. 102.
2 Alan Ecclestone, *Yes to God*, p. 77.
3 Cited by Catherine von Ruhland, *Prayers from the Edge: Meditations for Life's Tough Times*, SPCK, 1996.
4 Peter J. Gomes, *The Preaching of the Passion*, Forward Movement Publications, 2002, pp. 18–19.
5 Rowan Williams, *Ponder These Things*, p. 55.

An All-Embracing Love

1 J. C. Ryle, *Practical Religion*, London, 1900, p. 94.
2 Samuel Taylor Coleridge, *The Rime of the Ancient Mariner*.
3 Sister Wendy Beckett, *The Gaze of Love*, p. 70.
4 Fyodor Dostoyevsky, *The Brothers Karamazov*, p. 375.

Abandonment

1 Thomas Merton, *Contemplative Prayer*, p. 13.
2 Thomas Merton, *Honorable Reader: Reflections on My Work*, Crossroad, 1989, p. 39.
3 Thomas Merton, *Seeds of Contemplation*, p. 123.
4 Ignatius of Antioch, *Letters to the Romans*, 6, 1–8.
5 Thomas Merton, *Contemplative Prayer*, p. 84.
6 Alan Ecclestone, *Yes to God*, p. 4.

God's Call to My Freedom

1 Anthony Bloom, *School for Prayer*, p. viii.
2 Thomas Merton, *Contemplative Prayer*, p. 84.
3 Charles de Foucauld. Cited by Brother Kenneth, *From the Fathers to the Churches*, p. 165.
4 Thomas Merton, *Honorable Reader*, p. 39.
5 Thomas Merton, *Contemplative Prayer*, p. 84.

A Perpetual Surrender

1 Thomas Merton, *Contemplative Prayer*, p. 13.
2 Mother Mary Clare, *Encountering the Depths,* p. 13.
3 Dietrich Bonhoeffer, *The Cost of Discipleship*, SCM Press, 1959, p. 78.
4 St Ignatius of Antioch, *Letter to the Magnesians*, N. 2.
5 St Augustine of Hippo, *Sermons*, Sermon Guelf 3.
6 Thomas Merton, *Contemplative Prayer*, p. 12.
7 St Thomas à Kempis, *The Imitation of Christ*, Book 2, Chapter 1.

Dying of a Love That Looks Like Death

1 W. H. Vanstone, *Love's Endeavour, Love's Expense*, p. 59.
2 Charles de Foucauld, *Letters from the Desert*, trans. Barbara Lucas, Burns & Oates, 1977.
3 Karl Rahner. Cited by Dorothee Soelle, *The Silent Cry,* p. 133.
4 Mother Mary Clare, *Encountering the Depths,* p. 1.

5 Paul Tournier, *A Doctor's Casebook*, SCM Press, 1954, p. 227.
6 Pierre Teilhard de Chardin.

The Yes to God

1 Thomas Merton, *Contemplative Prayer*, p. 33.
2 Alan Ecclestone, *Yes to God*, p. 4.
3 R. S. Thomas, 'The Prayer', *Collected Poems*.
4 William Blake, 'To The Christians'.

Living and Dying with the Beloved

1 W. H. Vanstone, *The Stature of Waiting*, p. 95.
2 Dorothee Soelle, *The Silent Cry*, p. 177.
3 St John Chrysostom, *Homilies: 2 Corinthians*, Hom. 14.1–2.
4 Office Hymn at Lauds in Passiontide, St Mary's Abbey, West Malling.
5 Lancelot Andrewes, *Sermon: Good Friday 1597*.
6 R. S. Thomas, 'Sure', *Mass for Hard Times*, p. 53.

Through Deep Darkness

1 Thomas Merton, *Seeds of Contemplation*, p. 123.
2 St Mary's Abbey, West Malling.
3 R. S. Thomas, 'In A Country Church', *Collected Poems*.
4 Thomas à Kempis, *The Imitation of Christ*, Book 3, Chapter 3.
5 R. S. Thomas, 'Crucifixion', *Counterpoint*, p. 37.

My Whole Desire

1 Mother Julian of Norwich, *Revelations of Divine Love*.
2 St Ignatius of Antioch, *Letter to the Romans*.
3 Gerard Manley Hopkins, 'Easter'.
4 George Herbert, 'The Call'.